Coast to Coast
BBQ

America's
Best Recipes
2008

by Anne Kinne

Ithaca Press
3 Kimberly Drive, Suite B
Dryden, New York 13053 USA
www.IthacaPress.com

Cover Design	Gary Hoffman
Book Design	Gary Hoffman
Illustrations	Andrew Evans
Edited by	Erika Cooper
	Trisica Munroe

Manufactured in the United States of America

9 8 7 6 5 4 3 2 1

Library of Congress Cataloging-in-Data Available
Printed in the United States of America

Kinne/ Anne
Cooking/Barbecue Cookbook/ Grilling cookbook/BBQ cooking

ISBN   978-0-9798494-4-2

www.CoastToCoastBBQ.com

Contents

Acknowledgements

There are many to whom I am grateful for their assistance with this book. I would start with Joan Mayor, Rick Keyes, Trisica Munroe, and Erika Cooper at Ithaca Press, without whom none of this would have come to fruition. I am grateful to Joan for being willing to do this project a year after I initially presented it to her and for her patience as I learned the ropes.

I am also grateful to my cousin Diann Leach, who had our Auntie Winn and several of us cousins all at her house when the idea for a cookbook was born two years ago.

I would like to thank each and every cook who shared their recipes for this book – this would not have been what it is without your help! I am grateful to Anita Kilgore for being the inspired woman she is. In a conversation, she said to me, "You have recipes from coast to coast" and the title was born.

Dedication

I dedicate this book to Winnifred K. Schroeder, my Auntie Winn.

1

History

of

Barbecuing and Grilling

Anne Kinne

Before we had a word for it, well actually before we had words, Eza and Ug were barbecuing outside their prehistoric domicile. They were pretty smart, those two. They discovered that if they put the mammoth meat that Ug brought home, with the help of his buddies of course, over or near the fire that kept away predators, it cooked the meat and preserved it as well. Voila! Barbecuing was born.

The actual word "barbecue" is generally believed to come from a Taîno word, "barbacoa." No matter where the word came from, the lifestyle it has given the world isn't going away anytime soon. Some think that during the "golden years" of the 1950's, as Americans settled in after the war, the barbecue boom began. I would tend to agree with that because that's when the Baby Boom began, with people staying home, being prosperous, and enjoying life. People were moving into homes that had yards, either front or back, and they made use of them. Not only for the children they were having but for the entertaining they were starting to do.

Today, just slightly after the winter whoosh of holidays, you will find grilling, barbecuing and outdoor living equipment in just about every store. You now have at your disposal a myriad of items to buy to make your "summer of grilling and barbecuing" a most rewarding one. Grocery stores now carry patio furniture, grilling accoutrements, and dishware in all shapes and sizes. Let us not forget to mention the department stores, big box stores, hardware stores, party stores, clothing stores, and the huge number of web sites that offer all one would ever dream of wanting for their grilling pleasure.

2

Grilling Hints

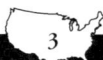
Anne Kinne

Indoor Grilling Tips

No outdoor barbecue or grill? No problem. You can achieve the same amazing results with a little modification of the recipes and the use of a few additional ingredients. There are a multitude of appliances and cookware available to make your indoor barbecue a complete success. Below are a few items that you will want to have on hand:

Liquid Smoke – This is a concentrated liquid available at almost all major grocery stores. When grilling indoors, use one teaspoon per one cup of oil to coat meat or fish. Then hand rub or toss with the dry rub spice mix. Be sure to use sparingly to taste! It is very concentrated.

Dry Smoke – This is a little harder to find, but makes an excellent addition to the dry rubs, or sprinkled sparingly over meat or fish. Again, it is concentrated, but not as much as the liquid smoke.

Dry Spice Rub – You can prepare your own or purchase a prepared Cajun Spice Mix.

Spices to consider: thyme, rosemary, ground cumin, oregano, ginger, coriander, kosher salt, and whole peppercorns.

Meat Preparation

A good quality dry rub is essential in preparing beef, pork ribs, or poultry for grilling or barbecuing. Once meat is thawed, rub with a mixture of oil and smoke and then the dry rub. Wrap in foil and refrigerate for four hours minimum. This mixture will infuse the meats, enhancing the barbecue result. This step is not recommended for fish or skinless chicken breasts.

Once cooking is complete, remove the meat from the container and place on a pan (If you made a foil container, open foil or take off the top foil layer). Heat your broiler to high, and place the barbecue under broiler to brown to desired finish. Flip barbecue and repeat on second side.

It is best to use a covered container and reduced heat when barbecuing pork, beef ribs or certain poultry and fish recipes. If large, covered containers are not available, you can use a good grade of aluminum foil along with a cookie sheet, pizza pan, etc. Extra wide aluminum foil is your best bet as it makes a great container. You will need a sturdy pan to hold the weight of the barbecue. Cover the pan with foil at least twice its length. Center the foil over the pan and add your prepared barbecue in the center. Fold up the foil on four sides and, if you have enough, bring the edges together and fold down in small increments on all sides. If there is not enough, add another piece of foil and fold together on all four sides.

It is important to make a sealed foil container around the barbecue.

Cooking Tools and Appliances

Grill Pan

Choose a grill pan if you have a small kitchen with little counter space for another appliance, but enough ventilation to handle a bit of smoke. If you like to use meat juices for sauces (which is not possible with most grills), this is an excellent way to capture these juices.

Best For: Thick cuts of meat like steaks, chicken breasts, and chops — the pan sits directly on a stove burner and gets hotter than the other grill types do.

Indoor Grill

Best known today as the appliance George Foreman made famous, these are basically an appliance with a base and folding lid that heats on both sides. The grills are usually slanted so that the juices flow away from the grill to a reserve container. This produces a "healthier" result by draining away the extra fats from the meats and coatings. They are now available in many variations and can also be found in combination with a panini grill. These units grill very quickly as they are designed to cook from the top and bottom—so check the temperature often, and be sure to adjust recommended cooking times for outdoor grilling accordingly. The liquids drained away during cooking can be preserved as the base for a sauce to serve over your meat. Scrape the leftover bits from the grill, after the meat or fish is done, into the reserved liquid. Put into a small saucepan on stove, slowly bring to a boil, and simmer to reduce by one half to one quarter.

Indoor Barbecue Pit or Rotisserie

An excellent appliance, these are now commercially available as a self-contained barbecue cooker, and some even have rotisseries included. Be sure that you have adequate ventilation wherever you choose to use the appliance and adjust your recipes to take into account use of liquid smoke and dry spice rubs.

Instant Read Thermometer

A "must have" tool for all grilling and barbecuing, this is a smaller thermometer, and the "Instant Read" provides a quick temperature check of your meat or fish. You do want to read the temperature as quickly as possible to reduce the amount of time you are in front of the heat. Be sure to use the recommended done temperatures for safe cooking.

Grilling and Clean-up

Always make sure you have adequate ventilation, especially with stovetop grills, or the top and bottom grill appliances available on the market. When you sear meat or fish that has been coated with oil and spices, you will produce smoke. This is a desirable result, but needs to be controlled with exhaust through the use of fans or open windows.

Indoor grills that have been used to cook meat or fish on high heat will build up a lot of browned or blackened bits of meat, or fish and spices on your pan, Teflon coated or not. These bits of meat or fish can be used as the base for excellent, savory sauces.

For non-stick pans, let cool and then scrape out the bits with a plastic spatula and save scraps for making a sauce, if you so desire. To make sauce: In a small pan, add a little water, wine, or fruit juice to the bits of meat, fish and spices, bring to a boil and then reduce to a simmer at the desired thickness.

If you are using a good grade stainless steel or cast iron pan, while still quite hot, add a small amount of white or red wine, water, or fruit juice depending on your recipe, and scrape the residue with a firm spatula to create a mixture of the liquid and bits of meat or fish and the spices. Simmer this to a desired thickness and it makes an excellent sauce to serve with your meat or fish. For a thicker, creamier sauce, add a tablespoon of whole or reduced fat milk.

Be sure to clean contact grills and grill pans while they are still warm. Once they cool, those browned bits are much harder to remove.

How to Easily Clean the Grill

One thing that is practically mandatory in grilling is to cook on a clean grill. You really do not want to be cooking pizza on the charred remains of last night's drumstick. Besides the flavor aspect of keeping a clean grill, you also want to consider the longevity of your grill. Keeping it clean will prolong its life. My gas grill is eight years old this season, which I think is pretty cool since it has traveled about 3000 miles with me.

When I get ready to cook, I turn the gas grill on high, close the cover, and go inside to finish preparing the food. A few minutes later, not more than five I'd say, I return to the grill and vigorously scrape the grill with a wire brush. I like the long handled models, so my skin doesn't come in close contact with that really hot surface.

While the grill is on, my friend Joan balls up some aluminum foil, spears it with a long handled barbecue fork and scrubs the dickens out of the surface of the grill. She's been doing that for years and swears by it. I've heard of putting a halved onion on a long handled fork to further clean the grill.

If you don't have a gas grill, not to worry. You can do the same procedure with a charcoal grill. Build your pile of charcoal right smack in the middle, light it, put the grill/grate on, close the cover and wait. Charcoal fires take, on average, a half hour to get ready. So before you throw your dinner on to cook, take a wire brush and scrape the heck out of it.

At the start of "the season," I completely dismantle the innards of the grill, remove the fake briquettes, and scrape away. Using an old spackle knife and copious amounts of paper towels, I scrape and scrape and scrape some more to clean the belly of the grill, the briquettes and any other part I can find. I also have a screwdriver handy so I can tighten up all the screws that have come loose during the last season. My grill has two wheels on it for easy maneuverability, and the screws seem to wiggle loose with use.

How to Make an Awesome Burger Patty

Believe it or not, there really is an art to making a good burger patty. Not that it will change the taste in any way, well it might, but a well made patty will make eating it a lot more pleasant. Let me tell you why: as I was growing up, we would have summer holiday cookouts at Uncle Kelly and Auntie Winn's. I actually don't remember who made the patties for grilling, but I do remember what they looked like after they were cooked. They weren't patties any longer. They were rounded balls of hamburger with a bun perched precariously on top. They tasted great, don't get me wrong. But what started out as a raw patty the size and thickness of the bun, shrank and ballooned into a ball when grilled.

This is what I've learned and how I like to grill a hamburger: I use 85% ground beef or chuck. I don't bother with the higher priced and less fat options. I'm a connoisseur of simple yet really yummy burgers. Ask any of my friends. Depending on how big the bun is that I'm using on any particular day, I make the patty just a smidge (that's my mother's technical term for just a bit bigger) bigger than the bun. Don't work the meat too much as you make the patty, and, as you form it, don't make it flat. This was Uncle Kelly or Auntie Winn's demise. In their defense, this technique probably wasn't invented yet. When the patty is formed to the desired width, press it a bit more in the middle, making a subtle "valley" of sorts. Don't make the famous Meteor Crater in Arizona or anything, just a noticeable subtle indentation in the middle of the meat. I think you'll be pleased with the shape and eating ease if you do.

Tips for Cooking Ribs

This is one of the most controversial subjects, with a lot of variations, opinions, styles, and a file full of experts. Well you know what, they are all right, and they all work. You will need to develop your own style and recipe combinations to perfect your own variations, opinions, and styles and become an expert in the rib arena. I am going to provide the basics here and go from there.

Pork Spareribs? Pork Baby Back Ribs? What is the difference? To keep it short, there are two layers to the rib. The top layer is what is called the baby back,

Anne Kinne

which is the smaller of the two, but with the more tender meat and more rib bones. The lower layer is what is known as the sparerib with a lesser amount of bones (sometimes none), that are larger with more fat around the meat and bones. The baby backs are the desired cut for most all barbecue rib recipes.

Prepare the ribs. Remove from the packaging and wash with a little water. Flip the rib rack over so the bottom is toward you. You will usually see a very thin membrane here that can be a little tricky to get a grip on it. I usually pinch it at one corner. Once you have it, pull back toward you at a 45 degree angle and remove as much of this membrane as possible. This initial small step will allow your ribs to stay flat, as the membrane has a tendency to shrink if not removed, curling the rack or ribs when you are in your finishing steps. It also makes the finished ribs much more tender.

Dry versus Wet Ribs?
Quite simply, the dry ribs are served as is, right from the grill. Wet ribs are basted with wet barbecue sauce during the final steps, and then just before serving. If you have never had dry ribs, try them. As a suggestion, cook the ribs dry and then serve the barbecue sauce on the side so all dry and wet rib fans can enjoy! When doing this, be sure to warm your sauce, but do not boil. Sauces contain a lot of sugar, and can burn under high heat, a desired result when basting, but not for your sauce.

After removing the membrane, be sure the ribs are moist, but not wet. The natural moisture of the rib is usually sufficient, but, if necessary, pat the rack of ribs with a wet towel. Add the dry rub mixture on all sides of the rack, and wrap in clear plastic wrap (foil can be used, but plastic wrap makes a better seal to keep air out) and place in refrigerator for four hours or more. Overnight is okay.

Remove from plastic wrap and, if smoking on a very low heat smoker, place rib racks on the smoking grate. Smoke for six to eight hours. If you are not using a smoker, seal in aluminum foil (you can place multiple racks of ribs in the same foil pack) and place on grill, or in oven, on low heat, 200 – 225 degrees F. for four hours minimum (more or less depending on the amount of ribs. If not enough here, you can make it up in the second stage).

Remove ribs from smoker or grill/ oven, and let sit for about 15 minutes to a half hour. Heat grill to high, and then cook racks of ribs on high, five minutes per side. Check for doneness with meat thermometer. Keep in mind that grill temperatures vary significantly so your cooking time needs to adjust accordingly. Watch closely so as not to burn the ribs, and keep away from direct flames. The rubs contain a lot of sugar, and sugar under high heat will burn. If you want a wet rib result, reduce the heat, baste the ribs with your favorite sauce, and then grill five minutes per side, basting while turning. Check for doneness, and baste one more time.

TIP!

To measure doneness, grab one third of the rib rack with a pair of tongs. Lift up and the other two thirds should begin to fall down at least by half if done. Confirm this with a meat thermometer!

The key here is to take your time, as you can see the preparation and process takes a commitment, but your satisfaction in your results will be well worth it. You are on your way to being an expert.

A Final Note Before You Get Started

I will be using the following abbreviations for all measurements in the book:

tsp = teaspoon
tbsp = tablespoon
Qt = quart
Qts = quarts

3

Cuts of Meat

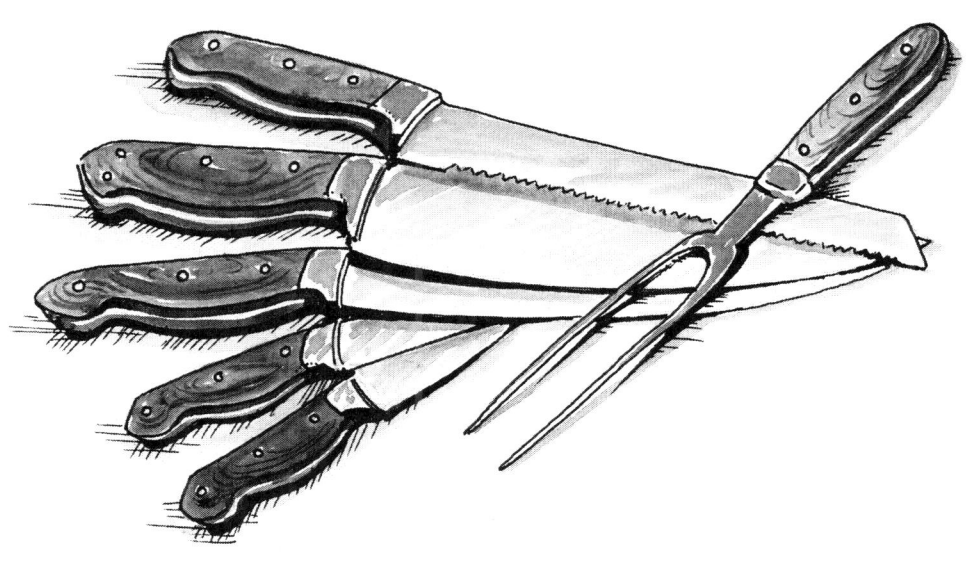

Anne Kinne

The following describes various cuts of meat that are typically used for steaks in grilling or barbecuing. The information below will give some descriptions of the cuts, as well as their various qualities.

The RIB or RIB-EYE

The prime (basic) rib cut (there are seven ribs to a side), can be divided into roasts or steaks, with or without the bone, and baby back or short ribs. The rib that contains a generous amount of fat is the high ticket item. This form of steak is also known as the Cowboy, or Rib-Eye steak.

Admired as the most satisfying of all beef cuts, the Rib-Eye is one of the most popular, juicy, and expensive steaks on the market. Meat from the rib section is tender and fattier (the meat is marbled with fat streaks throughout the cut) than other cuts of beef. This extra fat makes Rib-Eye steaks and roasts especially tender and flavorful.

The Rib-Eye can be cut boneless or bone-in. A bone-in Rib-Eye, often referred to as a Cowboy Rib-Eye or Cowboy Steak, is synonymous with a rib steak. The cuts are otherwise identical, and a justification sometimes used for leaving the bone in is that extra moisture and fat alongside the bone will enhance the flavor, although

the inclusion of the bone may also be used to inflate the weight of the steak. Many experts over the years have suggested cooking the rib steaks with the bone, to be eaten without utensils in true cowboy tradition.

FILET MIGNON

The filet is a steak cut from the tenderloin, of which there are only two per animal. When cut, the tenderloin portions become known as the Filet Mignon steak. The filet is considered to be the most tender cut of beef, as well as the most expensive.

Filet Mignon is normally cut two inches thick, and grilled as-is. As the filet has low fat levels, many wrap the Filet Mignon with bacon to add flavor. This also locks in the juices and keeps the steak from drying out during the cooking process.

When cutting the whole tenderloin, the end pieces are excellent for beef tips, which are quickly braised under high heat and then cooked under lower heat to desired doneness.

NEW YORK STRIP

The Strip Steak (also known as Striploin, Shell Steak, Delmonico, New York or Kansas City Strip Steak) is one of the highest quality beef steaks on the market. In British Commonwealth countries, this is called "Porterhouse

Steak," which has a different meaning in American English. Cut from the strip loin, the Strip Steak consists of a particularly tender cut. Unlike the nearby Filet Mignon, the Striploin is a sizable cut, more marbled, but is cut into the larger portions favored by many steak eaters.

When still attached to the bone, and with a piece of the beef tenderloin also included, the strip steak becomes a T-bone steak or a Porterhouse.

T-BONE / PORTERHOUSE

The T-bone and Porterhouse are steak cuts of beef. They consist of a T-shaped bone with meat on each side. One side has the meat known as the New York Strip or Strip Steak, which is the larger side, and the other side contains the tenderloin. Porterhouse steaks are basically the same as the T-Bone, but contain a larger portion of the tenderloin.

T-bone and Porterhouse steaks are generally considered to be one of the highest quality steaks, and prices at meat markets and steakhouses are accordingly high.

FLANK STEAK

The Flank Steak is a beef steak cut from the belly muscles of the cow. Long and flat, the Flank Steak's best known application is London Broil, a misnomer, as the dish did not originate in London. The popularity of London Broil has driven up the price of Flank Steak over the past few decades, but it is still one of the most affordable

steaks on the market. It is substantially tougher than the loin and rib steaks, therefore many flank recipes use marinades or moist cooking methods, such as braising.

It is quickly seared in a hot pan and eaten rare to maintain its tenderness. Strips of Flank Steak, known as arrachera, are very popular in Mexican cuisine and may be used to fill tacos, or served in large pieces as a main course. Flank Steak used in Mexican cuisine may be tenderized by a marinade, or by mechanical tenderizing, using a machine similar to that used to produce Cube Steak.

Flank Steak is best when it has a bright, red color. Because it comes from a strong, well-exercised part of the cow, it is best prepared when cut across the grain. Additional tenderness can be added by marinating the meat in a tenderizing liquid, including acids like tomato-based products, lemon juice, wine, vinegar, pineapple, papaya, or ginger.

CHUCK STEAK / ROAST

Chuck is best known for ground chuck, to many the most flavorful cut for burgers. It deserves recognition as more than burger meat, as it will yield many variable steak cuts.

The typical Chuck Steak is about one inch thick and contains parts of the shoulder bones, which is usually grilled or broiled; a thicker version is sold as a "7-Bone Roast" or "Chuck Roast" and is usually cooked with liquid as a pot roast (beef). The bone-in Chuck Steak or roast is one of the more economical cuts of beef.

Other boneless chuck cuts include the Chuck-Eye, Top Blade Steak, Under Blade Steak, Shoulder Steak and Roast, and Arm Steak and Roast. The average meat market cuts thick and thin Chuck Steaks and some meat markets will sell pot roast under the generic name "Pot Roast." The chuck contains a lot of connective tissue, including collagen. Collagen melts during the cooking of the meat, making the flavor intensely strong. Meat from the chuck is usually used for stewing, slow cooking, braising, or pot roasting.

4

Marinades and Sauces

Anne Kinne

R.L.'s Bar-B-Q Sauce

Sharon Slocum via Aunt Ginny and Uncle Lynn (Virginia and Lynn Freeman)
Sharon - Meridian, Idaho; Ada County;
Virginia Freeman - Montrose, California, Los Angeles County then, and Tenino,
Washington; Thurston County now

According to Sharon's Aunt Ginny, she and her husband Lynn had The Bar-B-Q Round-up in Montrose, California from 1958 to about 1970. It was a Texas style BBQ, and the meats were cooked with wood. Sharon's Uncle Lynn took a recipe from the Bar-B-Q Pit in San Diego where he worked in the early 1950's, changed it, and made it his own. Apparently, as family lore goes, he liked to change the recipe and did not follow it every time he made it. This recipe has been scaled down from the original restaurant recipe so that it is manageable in a regular kitchen.

Being raised myself in San Diego, I was very interested in the fact that the original recipe came from the restaurant Sharon's uncle worked at in San Diego. This would likely be the one that my own father had me go to at least once a week for the best ham and beef sandwiches ever! Six degrees of separation is at play here, as this recipe came to me via my cousin, Micaela Jones, who works with Sharon.

A special thank you to Sharon Slocum and her dear Aunt Ginny (Virginia Freeman) for contributing this particular recipe for the book! The world lost the creator of this sauce last year when Lynn Freeman passed away. I am grateful and fortunate to be able to pass it along in this book so it can be kept for generations to come.

(Teaspoons are rounded)
1½ tsp cayenne
½ tsp nutmeg
½ tsp cinnamon
½ tsp cloves
½ tsp paprika
½ tsp cuminos
¼ tsp dry mustard
¼ tsp (touch) garlic
6 bay leaves
½ cup vinegar
½ cup sugar (opt.)
1 cup water
1 #10 can or 3 Qts catsup
1.5 cans (28 oz) apple butter

Mix together spices, sugar, vinegar and water. Simmer 20 to 30 minutes.
Strain or remove the bay leaves.
Add catsup, mix thoroughly.
Add apple butter to mix.
Keeps in the refrigerator and can be frozen.

Lisa's Marinade for Chicken, Pork or Beef

Lisa Hartman
San Diego, California; San Diego County

Lisa and I used to go to the same church, First UU San Diego, before I moved to New Mexico. I always thought she dressed with flare and panache. I know her cooking conveys the same taste (Pun intended!).

1 cup soy sauce
1 cup raw cane sugar (or just sugar)
¾ cup onion, thinly sliced
½ cup sake
½ cup mirin (sweet sake wine)
1 tbsp garlic, minced
1 tbsp ginger, thinly sliced
½ tsp ground pepper
½ tsp dry mustard

Place in a large Ziploc™ bag with meat. Chill two hours or up to a day.
Grill meat and serve with grilled long green onions.

Anne Kinne

Uncle Ed Bowers' BBQ Sauce

Via Demi Bowers Morrow
Rose Lake, Minnesota *then* and Walnut Creek, California; Contra Costa County *now*

Ahh, those Minnesota Memories of many a family reunion on the lake. Garrison Keillor sure has it right with his Lake Wobegon Days.

Demi remembers: "I believe that dad talked to a chef in New Orleans about the recipe and then adjusted it to his own taste. He introduced it to the family after a trip to New Orleans in about 1940 or so. It was a special meal on holidays and for guests at our summer cottage at Rose Lake. Dad and my husband Jim often baked homemade French-style bread or sourdough to serve with the meal, as well as either coleslaw or potato salad. When Jim came home with me from college to meet my parents, we had only been in the house about an hour when mom and I checked out Jim and dad in the kitchen...Jim, with pencil and paper, was already being given the BBQ rib recipe."*

(Approximate measurements according to taste)
1 cup water
1 cup Heinz™ catsup
4 tsp dry mustard
¼ tsp red pepper
1 tbsp cider vinegar
1 tbsp Worcestershire sauce
1 tbsp brown sugar
½ tsp black pepper
1 to 2 tsp liquid smoke
½ tsp garlic salt
Dash of Tabasco™

Blend thoroughly. Serve extra at table. Keeps well.

Barbecue Sauce

Dolores Kinne Cameron
Nova Scotia, Canada

I never knew my Aunt Dolly. However, she was just as good a cook as the rest of her four sisters. You can find copious varieties of smoked salt on the Internet at places like saltworks.us; Williams-Sonoma.com; and Amazon.com. Who knew?

1 cup catsup
1 cup water
4 tsp dry mustard
6 tsp smoked salt
5 tsp garlic salt
½ tsp red pepper
1 tbsp vinegar
1 tbsp Worcestershire sauce

Combine ingredients in a pan on the stove, simmer for 15 minutes.

Anne Kinne

Garlic-Butter Sauce

Dar Stone
Albuquerque, New Mexico; Bernalillo County

Dar's a friend from "down south." A "Gourd Head" like me! This means we're gourd artists and good cooks too.

3 tbsp mayonnaise
2 tbsp grated parmesan cheese
1 lemon, juiced
¼ cube of butter (not margarine)
½ tsp garlic powder

Put all ingredients in microwaveable bowl. Stir well and microwave for approximately 30 to 40 seconds until butter is melted. Stir again and pour over grilled asparagus or place in small condiment bowl and place next to asparagus on the platter and let everyone serve themselves. Note: This is a great creamy topping for grilled, broiled, or baked fish, or on grilled asparagus or steamed broccoli.

Vinaigrette for Steak Sauce and Excellent Salad Dressing

Rick Keyes
Skaneateles, New York; Onondaga County

I haven't actually met Rick in person, but I can tell you I sure wish we lived closer. Read on for more of his yummy concoctions.

½ cup extra virgin olive oil
¼ cup shallots, minced
If you have access to truffles, ¼ cup, chopped
1 cup dry red wine
2 tbsp apple cider vinegar
1 tbsp thyme
Coarse kosher salt

Heat 1 tablespoon of oil in small skillet over medium heat. Add shallots and sauté for two minutes. Add truffles, sauté another one minute. Place shallot mixture in small bowl.

Boil wine in heavy small saucepan until reduced to 2 tablespoons, takes about ten minutes. Add to shallot mixture. Whisk in vinegar and thyme. Gradually whisk in remaining 7 tablespoons oil. Season vinaigrette to taste with coarse salt. Let stand at room temperature.

Barbecue Rub

Rick Keyes
Skaneateles, New York; Onondaga County

1 cup refined sugar
1 cup brown sugar
1 tsp cayenne pepper
½ cup coarse sea salt
2 tsp black pepper
1 tsp garlic powder
¼ cup paprika
2 tsp chili powder

Combine all ingredients and store in container. Use as a rub on any meat for barbecue.

Standard Barbecue Sauce

Rick Keyes
Skaneateles, New York; Onondaga County

1 cup brown sugar
2 cups catsup
2 cloves garlic, minced
2 tbsp molasses
½ cup minced onion
2 tsp vegetable oil
1 cup water
1 tsp mustard
2 tsp apple cider vinegar
½ tsp salt

Sauté garlic and onion in vegetable oil until soft and onions are clear, but do not brown. Add half of the water and all other ingredients. Simmer for 20 minutes, stirring occasionally. If sauce is too thick, add remaining water accordingly.

Sweet and Hot Barbecue Sauce

Rick Keyes
Skaneateles, New York; Onondaga County

1 cup brown sugar
2 cups catsup
2 cloves garlic, minced
4 tbsp molasses
½ cup onion, minced
2 tsp vegetable oil
1 cup water
1 tsp mustard
2 tsp apple cider vinegar
½ tsp salt
3 whole jalapeno peppers, diced
with seeds removed (Use gloves
when chopping jalapenos.)
¼ cup honey

Sauté jalapenos, garlic, and onion in vegetable oil until soft and onions are clear, but do not brown. Add half of the water and all other ingredients. Simmer for 20 minutes, stirring occasionally. If sauce is too thick, add remaining water accordingly.

Aunt Naomi's Marinade

Naomi Juvrud via Diann Juvrud Leach
San Diego, California; San Diego County via San Antonio, Texas; Bexar County

Now, I did know my Aunt Naomi, as she was one of the four sisters who eventually called San Diego their home. Aunt Naomi was a fantastic cook. We used to go to her house for holidays, and just be in seventh heaven. At some holiday gatherings, when she would have the whole family and friends come too, she and my mother would place "rounds" of cleaning chores in a hat and everyone who came to eat would pick out a chore. For example, there would be "Round 1" – washing, drying, and putting away the dishes; when those workers got tired, those that picked "Round 2" were up next to wash, dry, and put away the dishes. Aunt Naomi never chose a chore. She was always the "Overseer."

½ cup oil
¼ cup lemon juice
1 tsp paprika
1 tbsp Worcestershire sauce
Dash of Tabasco™
2 tbsp vinegar
2 tsp salt
2 tsp white sugar
Dash of garlic powder

"Drink it by the Gallon" Dressing

Scott Webb
San Diego, California; San Diego County

Christie, Scott's wife, loves this dressing so much she says she "drinks it by the gallon," and thus the name was created. Christie knows a good thing when she tastes it! Lucky for her, she has Scott around to create these delectable sauces and dishes! I absolutely love going over to their house for dinner – for the yummy food and to see the dearest two-year-old in the world, Adam.

1 cup extra virgin olive oil
½ cup balsamic vinegar
1 tbsp soy sauce
2 cloves garlic
⅓ cup fresh parsley

Mix all ingredients and let stand 15 minutes to a half hour to allow flavors to blend. Shake vigorously just before pouring. Great on salads, fish, meat, or just by itself, as Christie does. I've mixed it with blue cheese dressing on salad – yummy!

Gratia's Barbecue Sauce

Gratia Berggren via Dean Berggren
San Diego, California; San Diego County; via Denver, Colorado; Jefferson County

I knew my Aunt Gratia too. She was one of the four sisters who settled in San Diego.

⅓ cup onion, minced
3 tbsp butter
1 cup catsup
⅓ cup vinegar
2 tbsp brown sugar
½ cup water
2 tsp prepared mustard
2 tbsp Worcestershire sauce
⅛ tbsp salt

Sauté onion in butter in pan, add remaining ingredients, simmer covered for ten minutes.

Anne Kinne

Gratia's Basic Basting Sauce

Gratia Berggren via Dean Berggren
San Diego, California; San Diego County; via Lakewood, Colorado; Jefferson County

Makes 1 Qt
¼ cup oil
¾ cup onion, chopped
1 clove garlic, chopped
1 cup honey
1 cup catsup
1 cup wine vinegar
½ cup Worcestershire Sauce
1 tbsp dry mustard
1 ½ tsp salt
1 tsp oregano
1 tsp black pepper
½ tsp thyme

Heat oil in a saucepan, add chopped onion and garlic, cook until tender. Add all remaining ingredients and bring to a boil, stirring constantly. Cook another five minutes, very slowly. This all purpose sauce can be poured into jars, sealed and stored. Perfect for basting hamburgers, steaks, frankfurters, spareribs, chops and ham steaks.

Country Style Rib Sauce

Diann Leach
San Antonio, Texas; Bexar County

Diann is a great cook, just like her mother and aunts, although she doesn't like to admit it. By her own admission: "I'm more left brained, give me a recipe and I can follow it, but to come up with something original is hard. If it says do this, I do that." It was in Diann and her husband Jerry's home just about two years ago that the concept for this book was born. She may not think she's creative, but the creative energy abounds in their home!

1 tbsp butter
1 clove garlic, crushed
Sauté garlic in butter.

Add to that:

½ cup catsup
⅓ cup chili sauce
2 tbsp brown sugar
2 tbsp chopped onion
1 tbsp Worcestershire sauce
1 tbsp mustard
1 tsp celery seed
¼ tsp salt
Dash hot pepper sauce
3 thin lemon slices

Bring all ingredients to a boil, stirring often. When cooled a bit, can be placed in jars and stored in the refrigerator.

Blue Cheese Dressing

Diann Leach
San Antonio, Texas; Bexar County

Again, my statement about her creativity!

1½ cup mayonnaise
8 oz sour cream
¼ cup chopped ends of green
onions
3 to 4 green onions, finely chopped
¼ tsp garlic powder
¼ tsp salt
¼ tsp pepper
1 tbsp lemon juice
4 oz blue cheese

Mix together above ingredients. Store in tight jar. Goes well in place of mayonnaise on a blue cheeseburger, on a steak, or on salad. Ask Jerry, he knows!

Stampede "Hot Seat" Barbecue Marinade

Sandra Anderson
Calgary, Alberta, Canada

Chop very fine - Green Peppers, sweet red/yellow peppers, red onions, garlic (optional – chopped leek or shallots)
1 cup virgin olive oil
¾ cup soy sauce (No MSG)
1 cup sweet red vinegar (No MSG)
½ cup lemon juice (Grate the lemon peel and zest in as well!)
¼ cup Worcestershire sauce
¼ cup prepared mustard
1 tbsp black pepper (or lemon pepper)
1 tbsp sea salt (optional)
1 tbsp Louisiana Hot Sauce™

Marinate selected meat overnight. Make enough extra sauce to add to final serving dish.

Lemon Herb Sauce

Sandra Anderson
Clagry, Alberta, Canada

1 cup lemon juice
Zest of 2 lemons (I also add the rind)
1 tbsp celery salt (No MSG)
1 tbsp lemon pepper (No MSG)
1 cup virgin olive oil
½ cup water
1 cup sweet vinegar (No MSG)
Add to taste: Chopped marjoram, rosemary, thyme, onion (I prefer red onions), garlic, and dill.

Combine all ingredients and shake well. Use as marinade and basting sauce.

Bourbon Barbecue Sauce Recipe

Rick Keyes
Skaneateles, New York; Onondaga County

3 tbsp butter
3 tbsp canola oil
1 cup chopped onion
½ cup bourbon
3/4 cup catsup
½ cup cider vinegar
½ cup orange juice
½ cup pure maple syrup
¼ cup dark molasses, unsulphured
2 tbsp Worcestershire sauce
½ tsp coarsely ground black pepper
½ tsp salt

In a saucepan, melt the butter with the oil over medium heat. Add the onions and sauté until golden, about five minutes. Add remaining ingredients and stir to combine. Reduce heat to low and cook until thickened, about 30 to 45 minutes. Stir often.

Use as a barbecue sauce. Excellent served warm with salmon, other firm bodied fish, or grilled meats

Spiedies

Rick Keyes
Skaneateles, New York; Onondaga County

This is a recipe from the Endicott, NY area, which has a large population of Italian influenced cooking. Spiedie, which comes from the Italian "spiedo," meaning "kitchen cooking spit," are found only within the southern tier of New York on the Pennsylvania border, and Pennsylvania's northern tier. During the '40's and '50's, spiedies were cooked on outdoor grills, on the sidewalks in town and sold as a sandwich or snack. The popularity of the spiedie grew and now even has its own Spiedie Fest and Balloon Rally, which features a competition for the best spiedie of the year.

Spiedies started out made from lamb, which is an excellent choice. Evolution has shifted the base meat to pork as the more popular meat of choice, and today, with a more health conscious society, chicken is becoming very popular. You can also use beef, veal, bison, venison, etc. The base marinade and cooking is the same. Traditionally, spiedies are cut up into one inch by one inch cubes and then marinated in a tart sauce for three to five days. The meat (four to five pieces) is then placed on a skewer, and grilled until done. The meat is then removed and placed onto a slice of fresh Italian bread. The bread acts as a folded mitt to hold the meat. Some like extra sauce on the meat sandwich, but be sure you cook the sauce from the marinade and cool prior to using again. Spiedie salads are now becoming popular, slicing the meat into smaller pieces and topping your salad.

The Marinade (one of hundreds so feel free to be creative and modify to your liking)

One cup vegetable oil (olive oil is not recommended as its strong taste can overcome the recipe. Olive oil also gels quicker than corn and canola oils.)

¾ cup red wine or apple cider vinegar

1 tbsp sugar

⅛ cup lemon juice

4 cloves garlic, fresh and minced

1 bay leaf

1 ½ tsp oregano

1 ½ tsp basil

1 ½ tsp thyme

½ tsp coarse salt (sea salt is best)

½ tsp ground black pepper

¼ tsp cayenne pepper

¼ tsp mint leaves (optional)

The Meat

Two lbs of any of the following: lamb, pork, beef, chicken, venison, bison. You may even mix up the

pork, beef, and lamb for a variety. Trim as much fat as possible.
Cut meat into one inch cubes, or squares for chicken and some other cuts, as close to one inch thick as possible.

The Process
In a large bowl, mix all the marinade ingredients well.
Place meat into a one gallon or larger re-sealable freezer bag.
Cover meat with all of the marinade and shake to completely coat the meat.
Place in refrigerator for three days. During this time, take out bag and shake the mixture to stir the marinade and meat mixture.
After three days, +/- a day or so, remove the mixture from refrigerator and let stand at room temperature for two hours. Pour mixture in a strainer (colander works well) to drain liquid. Reserve liquid.
Remove bay leaf and discard.
Place four to six pieces of meat onto a skewer (metal preferably). If using wooden skewers, be sure to soak in warm water for 20 minutes just prior to using. You want about five inches of meat on each skewer to fit onto bread. When turning skewers, use tongs or oven mitt. The metal skewers will be very hot!
Pre-heat grill, and cook about three to five minutes per side (there are four sides) until done to your preference, basting with marinade while cooking.
While the meat is grilling, bring reserve marinade to boil, and then simmer on low for five minutes. Let cool.
Remove meat from grill, place skewered meat onto a piece of fresh sliced Italian bread, and fold bread around the meat and pull out skewer.
As a variation, for a larger sandwich, use fresh hoagie or sub rolls.

5

Grilled Veggies

Anne Kinne

Essential Grilled Veggies

Cathryne Richards
Placitas, New Mexico; Sandoval County

Cathryne is another gourd artist and friend. Incredible artistic and creative prowess this one has. Cathryne says:

"We have lots of friends who are vegetarian and this is a great hit either as a side dish or main course."

1 zucchini, cut into half inch slices
1 each red, green and gold bell pepper, sliced one inch thick
12 asparagus spears
12 mushrooms, quartered

Marinate in 1 cup of Paul Newman's Low Fat Ginger Salad Dressing™ for one hour. Place on grill and cook until tender. Using a skewer will help to keep veggies together.

Grilled Marinated Portobello Mushrooms

Cathryne Richards
Placitas, New Mexico; Sandoval County

Leave it to Paul Newman to have a yummy dressing that goes on so much that Cathryne and her husband Tom grill.

Marinate mushrooms in 1 cup of Paul Newman's Low Fat Ginger Salad Dressing™ for one hour.

Place on grill and cook until tender.

Grilled Stuffed Eggplant

Debbie Zeyher
Pecos, New Mexico; San Miguel County

Debbie is my accountant, though I am not sure where her true passion lies – with numbers or in the kitchen!

1 tbsp garlic, chopped
1 "big handful" of fresh basil – overstuff the eggplant because it will shrink
Olive oil

Cut an eggplant in half. Cut a trough in the middle of both sides and fill center with the garlic and basil. Drizzle olive oil over center of eggplant. Put the halves together and wrap in foil. Barbecue about 30 minutes if you place it on the side of the coals. 15 to 20 minutes if placed on top of the coals.

Grilled Asparagus

Dar Stone
Albuquerque, New Mexico; Bernalillo County

Dar says: "I blanch for three minutes in salted, boiling water, rinse in COLD WATER to stop the cooking and keep a beautiful green color, drain and set aside. I will grill over high heat for one-and-a-half minutes per side right before whatever else you are grilling is done. I like my asparagus firm so this applies to medium-thick asparagus. Thicker asparagus, if fresh, will take a bit longer, probably four minutes blanching and grilling two minutes per side. Thin asparagus, blanch for two minutes and grill about one minute per side. I often serve with my recipe for easy garlic-butter sauce." That is listed in the chapter on marinades and sauces.

Texarkana Veggies

Diann Leach
San Antonio, Texas; Bexar County – previously of Texarkana, Texas; Bowie County

In heavy-duty foil place:
1 green pepper, chopped
1 cup tomatoes
Onion slices (as many as you like)
Splash of Worcestershire sauce
Dot with butter
Salt and pepper

Fold securely and place on grill. Can make one large amount or break this into individual servings

Grilled Veggies with Couscous

Scott Webb
San Diego, California; San Diego County

As above, my cook cousin extraordinaire!

Eggplant
Mushrooms
Carrots
Red bell pepper
Tomatoes
Extra virgin olive oil

Wash, clean and cut all vegetables in thin, easily handled strips except the tomatoes – keep those whole. Put veggies in pan or bowl to drizzle and coat with oil. Place directly on grill, or on grilling tray. Watch closely as they don't take long to cook. Prepare couscous per box directions. When vegetables are done, cut into bite sized pieces. Add them to the couscous.

Grilled Portobello Mushrooms à la Schmoul

Schmoul
San Diego, California; San Diego County

Schmoul is the most wild of characters I know. His wife, Leesa, and I go back many years, BS (Before Schmoul). He's a "Dead Head," a mountain biker, a comedian, and a really good cook. He puts all the passion and creativity he has into his cooking.

Schmoul says: "With a spoon, scoop all the black stuff out of the inside, pat down to dry. The longer you cook it, the tougher it gets, you don't want it tough. But get the grill marks on either side."

Marinade
Extra virgin olive oil and balsamic vinegar (use about a 3 to 1 ratio)
Herbs de Provence (just a little)
Garlic, minced

Place the cleaned mushrooms in the marinade but don't soak them too much or for too long (they can get mushy). Place on grill for about four minutes

Altered Asparagus

Gratia Berggren via Dean Berggren
San Diego, California; San Diego County, although we cannot be sure if this recipe
pre-dates Aunt Gratia's San Diego days. It may have come from Wadsworth, Ohio;
Medina County via Lakewood, Colorado; Jefferson County
Altered by Anne Kinne
Pecos, New Mexico; Santa Fe County

1 lb fresh asparagus
¼ cup extra virgin olive oil
1 tbsp fresh parsley
3 tbsp vinegar
2 tbsp chopped pimiento
¾ tsp salt
¼ tsp pepper

Place asparagus in a small shallow dish. Combine remaining ingredients in a jar and shake vigorously, pour over asparagus. Cover and chill at least four hours. Place on grill and cook till desired tenderness.

6

Burgers

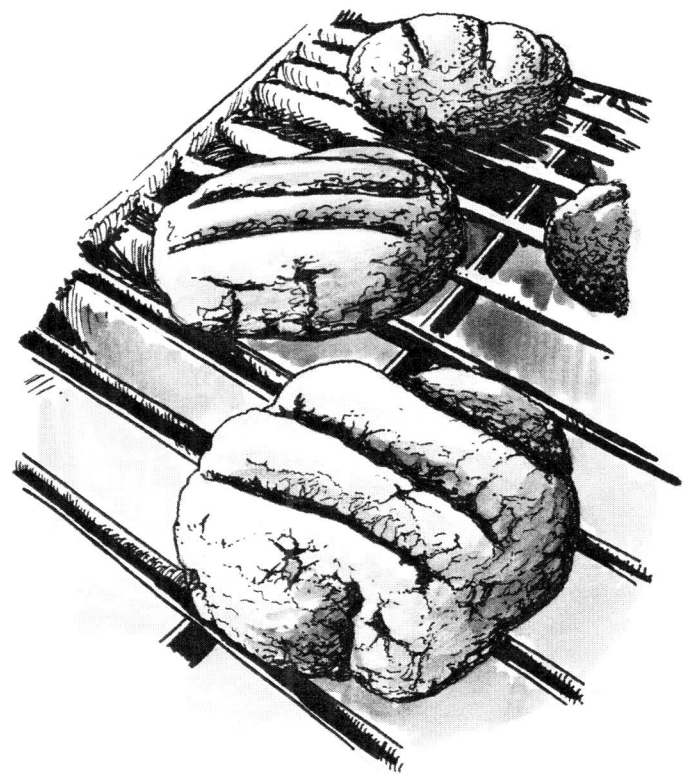

47

Blue Cheese Lovers' Cheeseburger

Anne Kinne
Pecos, New Mexico; Santa Fe County

Makes 3 to 4 burgers

1 lb ground beef
3 or 4 heaping tbsp crumbled blue cheese (one or more per burger)
3 or 4 slices Swiss cheese (one per burger)
Mustard (I prefer Sierra Nevada's Pale Ale Mustard™)
4 hamburger buns
Other garnish as desired

See notes on how to make an awesome burger patty.

Heat and clean grill. See notes. If using a gas grill, turn to low. Cook till desired doneness, five or more minutes per side, covered. When nearing completion, put blue cheese on the center of the burger. Cover with Swiss cheese. Cover grill, and finish cooking. This time will vary depending on how melted you like your cheese. Remove and enjoy.

I have found a very yummy taste combination between a good mustard and the blue cheese. Not any standard yellow mustard will do here. I'm not saying to go out and get the Cadillac of mustard, if there even is such a thing. But a nice, full bodied mustard blends so well. You'll be pleasantly surprised.

Since I am a cheese-a-holic, I add the Swiss cheese for more cheesy goodness. I always use Jarlsburg. To me, this is the Cadillac of Swiss! It has a pleasant nutty flavor, without being overwhelming. This cheese also blends well with blue cheese and good mustard.

Variations on a Cheese Lovers' Cheeseburger

Diann Leach and Anne Kinne
San Antonio, Texas; Bexar County and Pecos, New Mexico; Santa Fe County

Make two very thin patties. On one of them, place blue cheese crumbles. Top with the other patty and grill. Add more blue cheese and/or Swiss while cooking, as above. Place any cheese of your choice in the middle of two patties.

Grate your favorite cheese and mix in with the ground beef as you grill. It's a bit messy, but good!

Onion Lovers' BBQ Cheeseburger

Anne Kinne
Pecos, New Mexico; Santa Fe County

Makes 3 to 4 burgers

1 lb ground beef
½ cup onion, finely chopped (I prefer a sweet onion, like Vidalia or Maui, or a red onion)
¼ to ⅓ cup barbecue sauce of your choice
4 slices medium or sharp cheddar cheese (one per burger)
Salt and pepper to taste
4 hamburger buns (I prefer onion buns)
Other garnish as desired

Heat and clean grill. See notes.

Mix ground beef, onion, salt, pepper and barbecue sauce in a bowl till well mixed. Form into patties. See notes.

If using a gas grill, turn to low. Cook till desired doneness, five or more minutes per side, covered. When nearing completion, put cheese on the center of the burger. Cover grill, and finish cooking. This time will vary depending on how melted you like your cheese.

As an optional variation, try adding sliced, cooked bacon on top.

Garlic Lovers' Onion Cheeseburger

Anne Kinne
Pecos, New Mexico; Santa Fe County

1 lb ground beef
½ cup onion, finely chopped (I prefer a sweet onion, like Vidalia or Maui, or a red onion)
1 to 2 tsp garlic, finely chopped (or 1 to 2 tsp garlic salt)
4 slices medium or sharp cheddar cheese (one per burger)
Salt and pepper to taste (if using garlic salt, limit the amount of regular salt you include)
4 hamburger buns (I prefer onion buns)
Other garnish as desired

Heat and clean grill. See notes.

Mix ground beef, onion, garlic (or garlic salt), salt, and pepper in a bowl until well mixed. Form into patties. See notes.

If using a gas grill, turn to low. Cook till desired doneness, five or more minutes per side, covered. When nearing completion, put cheese on the center of the burger. Cover grill, and finish cooking. This time will vary depending on how melted you like your cheese.

Green Chile Cheeseburgers

Anne Kinne
Pecos, New Mexico; Santa Fe County

Since moving to Northern New Mexico, I have become acquainted with the green chile phenomenon that IS New Mexico. People here eat it with, and on, and in everything they can. The streets of many a New Mexico town are filled with the aroma of roasting chilies during the fall. It is a cultural wonder, this chile roasting season, a time honored tradition. If you ever consider a trip to New Mexico, come in the fall to experience this beautiful custom.

1 cup (or less – depending on their "heat") of fresh green chilies or if you don't have access to them, use 1 can diced green chilies
1 lb ground beef (makes 3 to 4 patties)
1 tsp garlic powder
Salt and pepper to taste
Cheese of your choice

Mix together chilies, ground beef, garlic powder and salt and pepper. Form into patties. See notes. Place on grill and cook till done, turning once. Place cheese (optional) on burgers during the last few minutes of cooking. Try putting more green chile over the burger when done and ready to serve. You'll feel like a real New Mexican.

7

Beef

Anne Kinne

Kalbi

Holly Lamonica
San Diego, California; San Diego County previously from the southern coast of South Korea.

Holly says: "In the mid '90's we were stationed on the southern coast of South Korea. We loved living there, but at first I was apprehensive about the food. When most Americans think of Korean food, they think of kim chee, which is usually fermented cabbage, white radish, chili powder, dried anchovies etc. I'm told there are about 300 varieties of kim chee and pretty much all of them are an acquired taste for the Western palate. Kalbi is a dish that is very palatable to Westerners, if they eat beef. It has wonderful flavor without being overpowering. Somehow, our family has come to associate this dish with special occasions or special dinners with friends. We first tried it at a restaurant when we lived in Chinhae, Republic of Korea. We enjoyed it so much that I asked a few Korean friends for their recipes. All were similar, but with distinct differences. One even included Coca-Cola™, which was intended to tenderize the beef. Since Coke has been found to remove paint, I suppose it was pretty effective. Others had honey or sugar in place of the pear juice. The recipe that I use is an amalgam of several. I usually serve kalbi with jasmine rice, Chinese cabbage salad (found in the side dishes section), steamed broccoli, and a fresh fruit platter."

Approximately 2 lbs of Korean short ribs, sometimes called Flanken Style. Choose the leanest you can find as they tend to be a fatty cut.

Marinate for several hours, and then grill. They will cook quickly as they are thin. Plan on about three ribs per person.

Marinade
½ cup soy sauce
½ cup crushed pear juice (available at Korean stores, or use ½ cup apple juice)
1 clove garlic or ½ tsp minced garlic
2 tbsp green onions, finely chopped
A few shakes of powdered ginger, or grated fresh ginger, if you have it
1 tbsp sesame oil

Marinated Flank Steak

Holly Lamonica
San Diego, California; San Diego County

Holly says: "I got the recipe from our pastor's wife, and then customized it a bit, adding the sesame oil and ginger. The coffee granules and the red wine combine to give more interest to the basic soy sauce flavor. Since flank steak tends to be leaner than other red meats, I was looking for recipes that would impart a more satisfying taste to a sometimes boring cut of meat."

1 ½ lb flank steak
½ cup soy sauce
2 tbsp dry red wine
1 tbsp instant coffee granules
1 clove garlic, minced
¼ tsp pepper
1 tbsp sesame oil
A few shakes of ground ginger and hot pepper sauce

Mix the marinade ingredients in a Ziploc™ bag. Score the flank steak at one inch intervals. Place the steak in the bag and marinate for several hours, then grill.

Anne Kinne

Steak on a Stick

Jan Christensen
Albuquerque, New Mexico; Bernalillo County

Jan is one of the best cooks in our family. She has been cooking all over the world as an officer's wife. I've seen her recipe books – there's like five of them! Jan says, "We ate a lot of bamboo sticks before I learned to soak before using!"

1½ - 2 lb. flank steak or top sirloin steak
½ cup sugar
½ cup soy sauce
¼ cup sherry wine or water
1 tsp ginger powder
1 tsp garlic powder

Marinate beef that has been cut into thin strips (beef should be cut against the grain) at least three hours. Place meat on bamboo sticks or skewers that have been soaked in water about a half hour. Barbecue a few minutes on each side. Great served hot or cold.

Teriyaki Steak

Winnifred Schroeder
San Diego, California; San Diego County up till about a year ago when she moved to
Lakeway, Texas; Travis County

Auntie Winn is another one of the family's great cooks, and an amazing woman.

½ cup soy sauce
¼ cup brown sugar
2 tbsp cooking oil
Scant tsp dry ginger
¼ tsp coarse ground pepper
Large clove garlic, minced or pressed
⅛ cup dry sherry
1 tbsp cornstarch

Mix well in flat glass dish — marinate steak at least four hours, turning occasionally.
Drain steak. Grill. Mix ½ cup water and 1 tablespoon cornstarch with marinade and bring to a boil. Serve with steak.

Anne Kinne

Matt's Kabobs

Matt Kilgore
Pecos, New Mexico; San Miguel County

Matt comes from a family of good and creative cooks. Look for his mother's, brother's and wife's recipes in future chapters.

8 large mushrooms
1 bell pepper, cored and seeded, cut into 8 squares
½ onion, cut into big squares
Butter
Garlic powder
Salt
Crushed red pepper flakes
12 oz boneless steak or chicken cut into one inch cubes

Place butter and garlic into pan with mushrooms. Sauté on low heat until mushrooms are golden brown, and then add the onion to pan. Sauté about five more minutes. Melt butter, and, in a small bowl, mix the butter, garlic, garlic salt, and crushed red peppers. Assemble kabobs by rotating sautéed mushrooms, onions, bell peppers and meat. Brush kabobs with mixture from the bowl and place on grill on low heat. Cook till meat is done, turning occasionally.

BBQ Steak Roast

Trisica Munroe
Ithaca, New York; Tompkins County

I haven't met Trisica yet, but I hope one day to be her best friend so she can invite me over for dinner every week. Stay tuned for several yummy recipes from her!

1 (5 lb) chuck steak, or other preferable cut
1 cup barbecue sauce
1 cup teriyaki sauce
1 (12 fluid oz) can or bottled beer
3 tsp garlic, minced
3 tsp fresh ginger root, thinly sliced
1 onion, finely chopped
3 tsp coarsely ground black pepper
2 tsp salt
2 tsp thyme
1 tsp roasted cumin seeds, ground

In a large bowl, mix barbecue sauce, teriyaki sauce, beer, garlic, ginger, onion, black pepper, thyme, cumin and salt. Place the roast into the marinade, cover and refrigerate for six hours, turning often. Preheat an outdoor grill for indirect heat. Remove the roast from the marinade, and pour the marinade into a saucepan. Bring to a boil, and cook for five minutes. Set aside for use as a basting sauce. Thread the roast onto a rotating barbecue spit above indirect heat. Cook the roast for two hours, or until the internal temperature of the roast is at least 145 degrees F. Baste often during the last hour with reserved marinade. Serve with mashed potatoes or oven roasted vegetables.

Anne Kinne

Grilled Pot Roast

Dave Kilgore
Santa Fe, New Mexico; Santa Fe County

Dave is Matt's brother, and a fisherman extraordinaire. See more of his recipes under seafood.

2 inch thick pot roast
Marinade in Kikkoman™ for two days

Sear it on both sides, on a hot grill. Reduce heat and cook on low temperature for 45 minutes to an hour and 15 minutes, depending on how you like it. Every time you flip it, add more teriyaki.

8

Pork

Anne Kinne

Grilled Sugared Ham

Debbie Thoene
San Diego, California; San Diego County

This recipe came through my old friend, Vicki Froistad. Vicki says: "The story behind this recipe was that I was staying with my in-laws when I had this ham. I was a little apprehensive when I found out how much horseradish was in it! Too spicy! But it was actually delicious and the horseradish didn't overpower it at all!"

2 fully cooked ham slices
1 cup brown sugar (packed)
⅓ cup horseradish
¼ cup lemon juice

Score each side of ham ¼ inch deep in diamond pattern. Combine remaining ingredients in small saucepan. Bring to a boil, stirring constantly.

Place ham slices on grill three inches from medium coals. Cook 15 minutes on each side, basting frequently with brown sugar mixture.
These can be broiled also and it works just as well.

Uncle Ed's BBQ Spareribs

Demi Bowers Morrow
Rose Lake, Minnesota *then* Walnut Creek, California; Contra Costa County

Good spareribs (about 1 lb per person)

Parboil and let cool to room temperature. Baste with his sauce (see recipe under marinades and sauces) and keep cool until ready to grill.

Baste and turn several times until well cooked.

Barbecued Spareribs

Dolores Kinne Cameron
Nova Scotia, Canada

3 lbs spareribs
1 cup water

Steam spareribs for 55 minutes in the water. Remove and place strips side by side. Cook 20 minutes on each side with two applications of barbecue sauce to each side. These may be baked, if preferred, in the oven about 1½ hours at 350 degrees F.

Variations on a Barbecued Sparerib Theme

Anne Kinne
Pecos, New Mexico; Santa Fe County

My cousin Diann taught me to cook spareribs 22 years ago. This is what I learned. Boil the ribs in a large pot with a couple of quarts of water (depending on how large your pot is and how many ribs you're doing). Cook about 45 minutes to an hour. Remove from water, place in shallow pan, coat with your favorite barbecue sauce. Place on grill and cook about five minutes on each side.

Pulled Pork Sandwiches

Rick Keyes
Skaneateles, New York; Onondaga County

Rick says: "The key with this recipe is to take your time, and enjoy the cooking process. There are three separate steps to a successful pulled pork barbecue sandwich."

Prepare the pork rub. Trim the excess fat from the pork and completely cover with the prepared rub. Let stand five to ten minutes. Smoke the rubbed pork a minimum of eight hours on a direct gas or direct heat smoker, though 12 hours is preferable over a low heat smoker. Do not disturb during the smoking process except to add wood or water to trays. Remove from smoker, and place the whole pork shoulder into a large crock pot. Add 1 cup water. Cook on low for another eight hours. If you do not have a crock pot, cook in covered dish in over at 200 degrees F for six hours.

Remove the pork from the crock pot (oven) and let stand for 15 minutes covered. You will then be able to pull the pork apart with your fingers, or, if still too warm, with two large forks. If you find that the pulled pork is a little dry, add small amounts of your favorite barbecue sauce or use your prepared sauce. DO NOT SATURATE THE PORK with sauce. You only want to keep it moist.

Keep warm and serve the pork with fresh rolls.

* If no smoker is available, put rubbed pork shoulder in oven container (foil oven trays and aluminum foil works fine). Add 1 cup water and 2 tbsp of liquid smoke to container and mix well. Pour into oven container and cover meat. Cook in oven for eight hours at 250 degrees F. Remove from oven and follow above directions from there.

5-Star BBQ Ribs

Trisica Munroe
Ithaca, New York; Tompkins County

1 cup Adobo™ seasoning salt
(recommended brand)
1 cup garlic powder
1 cup black pepper
1 large rack pork spareribs, about 6
lbs
1 to 2 bottles Jack Daniel's BBQ
Sauce™ (recommended brand)

Prepare grill. Mix seasoning salt, garlic powder and black pepper together. Rub onto ribs. Place rack of ribs, rib side down, onto grill and cook for 15 minutes. Turn ribs over and cook for another 15 minutes. Remove ribs from grill just before being cooked to your liking. Empty barbecue sauce into roasting pan and let heat for five to seven minutes. Transfer ribs to sauce, cover and let cook for another 10 to 15 minutes. Serve ribs with sauce on the side.

Smoked Baby Back Ribs à la Schmoul

Schmoul
San Diego, California; San Diego County

Schmoul says: "First you need a smoking jacket – something to smoke in."

Use a smoker – must have indirect heat. Skin the ribs, take all the inside membrane off, it makes them more tender. Ask the butcher to do this. Or, you can do it yourself by making a cut with a sharp knife down the membrane, and just pull it off.

Season with any kind of rub you like at the time. One of Schmoul's favorite blends is cayenne pepper and a brown sugar base. He encourages everyone to try and experiment with different pork roasting rubs. Coat both sides with extra virgin olive oil to hold the rub on, massage it in, and get intimate with your ribs.

Get the smoker going. Schmoul likes hard wood such as apple, pecan, or oak. An offset fire box pulls the smoke through the ribs, and this is a good thing. Every time you open it, the heat escapes. Build a fire, and resist the temptation to open the smoker and lose the heat. While the ribs are smoking, they must be rotated. Those ribs closer to the fire box cook faster than those far away. Every 20 minutes or so, rotate. The fire should not be above 200 degrees F. Smoke for eight to ten hours, letting the fire burn out. No sauce is needed.

9

Chicken

Anne Kinne

Grilled Chicken and Veggie Kabob

From Cathryne Richards
Placitas, New Mexico; Sandoval County

1 zucchini, cut into half inch slices
1 each red, green and yellow bell
pepper, sliced one inch thick
12 asparagus spears, cut in about
two inch slices or so
12 mushrooms, quartered
2 to 3 skinless boneless chicken
breasts cut into one inch cubes
Bamboo skewers soaked in water a
half hour or metal skewers

Marinate in 1 cup of Paul Newman's
Low Fat Ginger Salad Dressing™
for one hour. Alternate threading
zucchini, peppers, asparagus,
mushrooms, and chicken on
skewers. Place on grill, rotate several
times to cook all sides until tender.

Garlic Sesame Chicken

Debbie Zeyher

Boneless, skinless chicken breasts in a large plastic bag
1 tsp garlic, chopped (from jar)
1 tbsp onion, chopped and dried
2 tbsp sesame oil
¼ cup Braggs™
1 tbsp lime juice
1 tsp ginger (optional), chopped

Mix together – leave at room temperature for at least two hours.

Prepare grill. Place on barbecue, cook until done.

Spicy Mustard Chicken

Debbie Zeyher

¼ to ½ cup spicy mustard of your choice (try some with horseradish in it)
1 tbsp Braggs™
2 tbsp lime juice

Mix ingredients together. Baste chicken while cooking. Barbecue till done.

Beer Can Chicken

Rick Keyes
Skaneateles, New York; Onondaga County

1 whole chicken, 3 to 5 lbs
2 tbsp olive oil
4 tsp seasoned pepper (a combination of black and cayenne peppers and paprika is great)
1 tbsp garlic, minced
Beer (non-alcoholic beers work fine), root beer adds a wonderful taste also
Dash of rosemary
1 "Beer Can" roaster (you can find these at sporting and outdoor stores. I found mine at Target™)

Prepare grill. Rub the chicken with the olive oil and sprinkle evenly with 3 tsp of seasoned pepper. Don't forget to lift the wings when you do this. Sprinkle rosemary, garlic and remaining pepper onto the skin of the chicken. Carefully place chicken on the roaster on the grill. Cook 30 to 35 minutes. Check the internal temperature of the chicken using a thermometer. Be sure to test both the breast and the thigh of the chicken near the bone. It should reach an internal temperature of 165 to 170 degrees F.

Chicken on Skewers

Diann Leach
San Antonio, Texas; Bexar County

Bamboo skewers soaked in water about a half hour before using
One de-boned chicken breast makes about two skewers

Whisk together:
One envelope instant meat marinade
¼ cup soy sauce
¼ cup dry cocktail sherry
¼ cup water
¼ cup sesame or corn oil
1 green pepper, cut into one inch pieces
1 onion, cut into one inch pieces

Thread chicken onto skewer. Add vegetables on ends or alternate with meat. Brush with marinade. Cover and put into the refrigerator until ready to grill. Brush with marinade during cooking. Cook four to five minutes on each side or until done. Turn only once. This is good with a rice side dish.

The "Cornell Barbecue Chicken Sauce"

Submitted by Rick Keyes
Skaneateles, New York; Onondaga County

The "Cornell Sauce" has a long history, developed at Cornell University's Farm Home Extension in the 1950's. The basic recipe has remained the same with very few variations. As you use this sauce over time, you will develop your own deviations to taste.

1 cup vegetable oil (Olive oil is a little strong for this recipe)
2 cups apple cider vinegar
2 eggs
1 tsp black pepper
3 tsp salt
1 tsp poultry seasoning
Recipe is enough for two whole chickens or one turkey.

Whisk all ingredients together, or use a blender. This creates an excellent emulsion.

Marinate chicken in sauce for one to two hours (overnight is good), and baste while grilling. Do not add sauce during the last few minutes of cooking, and be sure the sauce and chicken is fully cooked. A meat thermometer should read 180 degrees F as close to the bone as possible.

Anne Kinne

Honey Marmalade Chicken

Sharon Cordova and Anita Kilgore
Farmington, New Mexico; San Juan County and Pecos, New Mexico; San Miguel County

Believe it or not, this yummy recipe was created on the phone by this mother and daughter team. Talk about creativity! The first time this recipe was made, it was in my very own kitchen. Anita and I forgot an ingredient, but it turned out just fine! We made a lot and leftovers were still scrumptious.

1 cup honey
⅓ cup orange marmalade (Anita suggested trying apricot)
3 tsp chipotle powder or flakes
¾ tsp garlic powder
½ tsp cinnamon
Salt and pepper
4 skinless boneless chicken breasts (can also be used with other chicken parts)

Wash and pat the chicken dry. In a bowl, mix together the honey, marmalade, chipotle, garlic and cinnamon. Reserve ⅓ of the mixture aside. Pour the rest into a Ziploc™ baggie, add chicken, close, and marinate for at least a half hour, not more than an hour in the refrigerator. Heat and clean grill. Place chicken on grill on low heat. Turn occasionally and baste with remaining marmalade mixture. Cook till done. Goes well with basmati rice.

Coffee Flavored BBQ Chicken

Trisica Munroe
Ithaca, New York; Tompkins County

12 pieces skinless chicken
½ cup butter
½ medium onion, finely diced
1 large garlic clove, minced
2 tbsp lemon juice
½ tbsp wine vinegar
½ cup barbecue sauce
¼ cup brewed coffee (any strong brew will do)
1¼ tsp salt
1 dash Tabasco™ sauce
1 tbsp Worcestershire sauce

Melt the butter in a small saucepan. Add onion, garlic, lemon juice, vinegar, barbecue sauce, coffee, salt, Tabasco™ sauce and Worcestershire sauce. Stir to mix well. Brush chicken pieces with sauce and barbecue over a medium hot fire. Turn and baste every five to ten minutes, until cooked through.

Thai-Style BBQ Chicken

Trisica Munroe
Ithaca, New York; Tompkins County

2 lbs boneless chicken breasts cut into strips
4 large sweet peppers
4 large green apples, sliced
3 large onions
Skewers (if bamboo, soak in water about a half hour before using)

Marinade
2 cloves garlic, chopped
1 tbsp curry
1 tsp coriander powder
1 tsp salt
1 tsp butter
3 tbsp light cream
½ cup coconut milk

Sauce
1 tbsp brown sugar
2 tbsp peanut oil
1 tsp lemon juice
½ tsp curry
½ cup barbecue sauce
Dash of chili/ hot sauce

Mix marinade ingredients together and add chicken to mixture. Cover and refrigerate for two hours. Chop peppers, onions, and apples into medium-sized pieces and set aside. Mix sauce ingredients together and simmer over low heat. Remove chicken from marinade and place on skewers, alternating with pieces of pepper, onion, and apple. Baste chicken and vegetable pieces with sauce, and roast over medium fire until cooked.

Lemon-Ginger Chicken

Trisica Munroe
Ithaca, New York; Tompkins County

3 to 6 chicken breasts
2 tbsp oil
½ cup onion, chopped
2 tbsp garlic, chopped
1 whole ginger, chopped
½ cup water
4 tbsp lemon juice
5 tbsp barbecue sauce
1 tbsp paprika
1 ½ tsp salt
1 tsp cumin
1 tsp ground coriander
1 tsp garam masala
½ tsp cayenne pepper
1 tbsp brown sugar

Season chicken with salt, paprika, coriander, cayenne pepper, cumin, and garam masala. Let sit for one hour. Sauté garlic and onion in oil over medium heat. Add ginger and water to blender and grate for three to five minutes. Strain out pulp using a sieve and preserve juice. In a small bowl, add ginger juice, lemon juice, barbecue sauce, and brown sugar. Mix well. Barbecue chicken over medium fire, basting with sauce often, until cooked.

Anne Kinne

10

Seafood

Anne Kinne

Ayame's Salmon

Via Phyllis Chinn
Arcata, California; Humboldt County

Phyllis was a good friend to me when I attended Humboldt State University, where she is still a professor. She remembers: "Ayame Tsutakawa was the wife of an internationally known sculptor, George Tsutakawa. They were the parents of my brother-in-law's wife.

Ayame was a typical Japanese wife in a Seattle setting — tremendously gracious, supportive of her husband and children, and a good cook. She took care of a large house, four children who lived near them, and several grandchildren."

Salmon steak
Mayonnaise
Soy sauce
Thinly sliced rounds of lemon
Aluminum foil

Place salmon steak on the foil, spread liberally with mayonnaise and a bit of soy sauce, top with thin rounds of lemon. Wrap foil tightly and place on barbecue until the foil puffs up and the fish is pink. Can also be cooked in the oven.

Dar's Plank-Grilled Salmon

Dar Stone
Albuquerque, New Mexico; Bernalillo County

2¼ inch cedar planks, pre-soaked for one hour in:
½ cup water
1 bottle of beer

4 thick salmon filets with skin removed

Glaze/Marinade
Stir ingredients together
¼ cup brown sugar
2 tbsp soy sauce (low salt)
¼ cup of apple cider (apple juice will work)
½ cup maple syrup

Marinate salmon for 15 to 30 minutes. Place on pre-soaked cedar plank. Season with lemon pepper. Preheat grill on high. Place on highest grate not directly over heat. Brush one side with more glaze and cook seven to ten minutes, depending on thickness of salmon with grill top closed. Flip salmon over on cedar plank, brush with glaze and cook seven to ten minutes on second side. With thinner filets, Dar brushes with glaze several times during the cooking. She serves this with grilled asparagus (see the chapter on veggies), green salad with miso dressing and crusty French bread. This recipe works equally as well with lobster (I brush the lobster with melted butter before serving) or swordfish steak. Salmon can be cooked directly on the grill but reduce the heat to medium and wipe grill with non-stick spray prior to cooking. With this method, the glaze has more "crackle" to it.

Lisa's Barbecue Shrimp with Pineapple

Lisa Hartman
San Diego, California; San Diego County

Lisa recalls: "A very good friend of mine, Marcia Biller, from First UU San Diego, called me one day and said I had to try this marinade. She said that her small family of three ate all the shrimp, and she was amazed she ate so much. So when I say it serves three, that's because it is devoured with gusto! I use only this recipe when I grill shrimp. I added the pineapple, because it is so pretty next to the pink shrimp." That's Lisa with her eye for color!

Serves three

2 lbs of fresh shrimp, shelled and de-veined
Place shrimp in a bath of 1 tablespoon each of sugar and salt. Place in refrigerator for a half hour. Pineapple, cut into one inch cubes.

Marinade
⅛ cup olive oil
Zest of 1 lemon
4 garlic cloves, chopped
2 tbsp parsley

Drain shrimp from bath and pour marinade over them. Skewer them with one inch size chunks of pineapple and barbecue quickly.

Dar's Planked Lobster or Swordfish

Dar Stone
Albuquerque, New Mexico; Bernalillo County

Do you get the idea that Dar likes to cook with planks?

For the lobster, Dar cuts down the middle of the "belly" membrane, turns it belly-side down on the plank and covers it with foil. I don't remove the lobster from the shell until after it is cooked (15 to 20 minutes). This keeps the lobster moist. You can cook lobster this way without the glaze. The plank really does give it a subtle, woody taste. YUM!

For the swordfish, she buys the steaks precut (about ¾ inch thick) and cooks it exactly like salmon.

Anne Kinne

Grilled Fish

Rick Keyes
Skaneateles, New York; Onondaga County

4 (6 oz) dense fish steaks, such as halibut, swordfish, shark or tuna
½ cup vegetable oil
2 tbsp red wine (medium dry sherry or cooking sherry)
1½ tsp ginger root
1 tsp orange rind, freshly grated
½ tsp lemon rind, freshly grated
3 tbsp soy sauce
Fresh ground pepper to taste

Arrange the steaks in a shallow dish. Whisk the rest of the ingredients until creamy. Pour the marinade over the fish. Marinate, covered, for two hours or overnight, turning periodically. Heat the grill until hot and brush with additional oil. Grill the steaks over high heat on both sides according to thickness (about ten minutes).

Grilled Wild Salmon

Scott Webb
San Diego, California; San Diego County

Scott states: "I prefer wild salmon, rather than farm raised that may have been fed artificial ingredients. I like organic foods."
"Why organic?" I ask him.
"I prefer to go out to my own garden and pick the garlic and other ingredients I cook with. It is healthier. I also prefer to cook salmon with skin on. Cooked skin is yummy and crispy." That's my cousin Scott!

1 lb wild salmon (feeds two)
¼ cup soy sauce (try Tamari in place of soy sauce)
1 to 2 cloves of garlic
1 cup olive oil

Cook salmon till it's done. The bigger/thicker it is, the longer it will take. Flip when the top looks like it's beginning to cook, and the sides look like they are beginning to cook too. Touch it. When it feels firm to the touch, it's done. Cutting it open also confirms it's done.

Grilled Wild Salmon Take Two

Scott Webb
San Diego, California; San Diego County

1 lb wild salmon
1 cup extra virgin olive oil
¼ cup soy sauce
2 cloves garlic, minced
1 tbsp ginger, sliced very thin
¼ cup parsley, finely chopped

Mix the oil, garlic, ginger and parsley together. Place salmon in pan, pour mixture over and let stand for 15 minutes or so. Can be placed in the refrigerator while you heat and prepare grill. Place salmon on grill, skin side down. Flip once when the top and sides look like they're beginning to cook. Baste with more of the marinade. Cook till done.

Grilled Shrimp

Scott Webb
San Diego, California; San Diego County

1 lb large shrimp, peeled and de-veined (optional). Scott does this after they're cooked.
1 cup extra virgin olive oil
¼ cup soy sauce or Tamari
2 cloves garlic, finely minced

Soak shrimp in marinade for at least 15 minutes, up to a half hour. Place on grill, turning frequently. Baste shrimp with extra marinade for extra flavor.

Grilled Shrimp Take Two

Anne Kinne
Pecos, New Mexico; Santa Fe County

1 lb large shrimp, peeled and deveined
½ to 1 whole stick of butter (may not need all of it, but better to have too much than to run out!)
4 to 5 cloves of fresh garlic, finely chopped
Dash of salt

Melt butter in large pan along with the garlic and salt. Add shrimp and begin to marinate over low heat for five minutes or so. Remove from stove and place on grill. Continue to baste the shrimp with the garlic butter until the shrimp are done.

Bacon Wrapped Grilled Shrimp

Anne Kinne
Pecos, New Mexico; Santa Fe County

I love bacon and add it to just about anything I can.

1 lb large shrimp, peeled and de-veined
Half as many strips of bacon as shrimp
¾ stick of butter
2 cloves of garlic, minced
2 tbsp lemon juice (optional)
Skewers (if using bamboo, soak in water for a half hour before using)

Slowly melt butter and add garlic. Do not allow to burn. Simmer to allow flavors to blend. Cut bacon strips in half. Wrap each shrimp in bacon, place on skewer. Place on grill and liberally baste with garlic butter sauce, turning until done.

BBQ Salmon Steaks

Trisica Munroe
Ithaca, New York; Tompkins County

6 to 8 salmon steaks (thawed)
1 cup plain yogurt
1 tbsp lemon juice
2 tsp ground cumin
1 tsp cinnamon
1 tsp cayenne pepper
2 tsp ground black pepper
1 tbsp minced ginger
2 tsp salt

1 tbsp butter
1 clove garlic, minced
1 medium onion, thinly sliced
¼ cup fresh cilantro, chopped
2 tsp cumin
½ tsp salt
½ cup barbecue sauce
¼ cup heavy cream
¼ cup cashew nuts (halves and pieces)

In a large bowl, combine yogurt, lemon juice, 2 tsp cumin, cinnamon, cayenne pepper, black pepper, ginger, and 2 tsp salt. Mix well. Pour mixture over salmon steaks, making sure to evenly coat pieces. Cover and refrigerate for two hours.

Melt butter in large skillet over medium heat. Sauté garlic, onion, and cashews for one minute. In a separate saucepan, over medium heat, add barbecue sauce, heavy cream, 2 tsp cumin, and ½ tsp salt. Simmer on low heat until sauce thickens, about 20 minutes. Individually wrap salmon steaks in foil, baste with sauce, and barbecue over medium hot fire. Turn packets every five to ten minutes until fully cooked. When ready to serve, garnish with cilantro and sautéed garlic, onion and cashews.

Spicy Grilled Shrimp

Trisica Munroe
Ithaca, New York; Tompkins County

1 lb shrimp
20 wooden skewers, soaked in water
½ cup soy sauce
4 tbsp oil
2 tsp salt
2 tsp black pepper
3 shallots, diced finely
2 cloves garlic, minced
1 (28 oz) can whole, peeled
tomatoes, drained and hand-crushed
2 tbsp malt vinegar
1 tbsp chili powder
¼ cup brown sugar
Lime wedges, for garnish

Thread shrimp onto skewers and place in a shallow dish. Pour soy sauce and 2 tablespoons oil over shrimp. Season with salt and black pepper. Set aside and let marinate for 30 minutes.

Heat 2 tablespoons oil in large pan over medium heat. Add shallots and garlic and sauté for one minute. Stir in tomatoes and season, to taste, with salt and black pepper. Add chili powder, sugar, and malt vinegar. Cook about 10 to 15 minutes, or until mixture has thickened.
Heat grill and cook shrimp for about three minutes per side. Garnish with lime wedges.
To serve, spread some barbecue sauce onto a large platter and place skewers on top of that.

Schmoul's Seared Yellowfin Ahi Tuna Steak

Schmoul
San Diego, California; San Diego County

Fresh Yellowfin Ahi steak
Chef Paul Prudhomme Blackened
Redfish Magic Seasoning™ (found at
www.chefpaul.com)
Butter
Cast iron skillet

Melt the butter in a smokin' hot skillet (best done outside on top of a gas grill). Coat both sides in butter, and liberally apply Chef Paul's seasoning. Cook one minute on each side, sear it, and keep it raw inside. That's it! Eat immediately. Don't take the time to slice it! Goes well with a little bit of lemon.

Fisherman Dave's Trout and Salmon

Dave Kilgore
Santa Fe, New Mexico; Santa Fe County

Dave loves to fish. I mean, he really loves to fish. He goes all over the state to do this, sometimes staying away for as long as a week. You should see his house, full of things only a devoted fisherman would truly appreciate. He even has a bathroom completely outfitted with fishing memorabilia and art.

Grilled Trout

Clean it first (now remember, Dave gets his fish direct from the lake, you can just go to your local store to buy it, if you're not a fisherperson).
Dave leaves the skin on (see below)
Place in foil
Garlic salt to taste
Dab with butter

Place wrapped fish on grill and cook ten minutes each side, until done.

Grilled Salmon

Clean it first (or go to your store and buy it already for you)
Place in foil
Squeeze fresh lemon
Dab of butter

Place wrapped fish on grill and cook till done, about ten minutes or more. When you open the foil, the skin sticks on the foil and is removed! Dave doesn't like the skin.

Simple Grilled Lobster Tail

Anne Kinne
Pecos, New Mexico; Santa Fe County

Cut the "top" of the tail down the middle with a sharp knife. Place cut side up on the grill, not directly over fire, and cook till the meat is done. It will burst through the cut in the shell, and open somewhat as it does. No need to turn or otherwise move the tail until it is ready to be enthusiastically eaten. Serve with melted butter.

11

Pizzas
and Paninis

Anne Kinne

Dar's Peppers and Pork Panini

Dar Stone
Albuquerque, New Mexico; Bernalillo County

Dar tells me: "You sure are a lot of trouble! Just kidding about the trouble since I want to include them in my family cookbook anyway. I have had to 're-construct' a lot of the old family favorites since I really don't use recipes per se. I hope I did okay. The SW Rueben is my all-time favorite. Once you prepare these, they are a snap, great for summertime cooking outside and can accommodate all types of fillings. I am still experimenting with different fillings. I made a teriyaki shrimp with water chestnuts that was pretty good but not as good as the Rueben." Dar is a great cook. She also gives me a lot of grief. Just kidding, Dar!

2 slices of thick (3/4 inch) artisan bread
2 ⅛ inch slice of low-moisture mozzarella cheese
6 oz cooked pork loin, shredded

Sandwich Filling
½ cup red bell pepper, thinly sliced
½ cup green bell pepper, thinly sliced
½ cup white onion, thinly sliced
¼ cup pickled banana or Italian yellow peppers, sliced and drained
½ cup mushrooms, sliced
Salt & pepper to taste
Extra virgin olive oil

Sauté peppers, onions, mushrooms over medium heat in 4 tablespoons of olive oil until browned but not mushy and set aside. Pre-heat grill to medium. Brush lightly one side of bread slice with olive oil and place on grill with bacon press on top until brown with dark grill marks. Remove bread slices from grill and fill with pork, peppers and mozzarella slice. With toasted side to the inside, assemble sandwich in this order:
Cooked pork
Mozzarella slice
Sandwich filling
Mozzarella slice
Place second slices of bread on top and brush lightly with olive oil. Using bacon press on top, grill on each side until golden brown. Serve hot. Notes: Cooking time will vary depending on how high you place your grilling surface. This works equally as well with cooked roast beef or chicken breast. For an all-veggie sandwich, sauté a whole Portobello mushroom to replace meat, and add a cup of julienne zucchini and eggplant to the sautéed sandwich filling. "It's all good," she concludes.

Dar's Southwest Rueben Panini

Dar Stone
Albuquerque, New Mexico; Bernalillo County

2 slices of thick (3/4 inch) rye bread
2 slices of Swiss or Havarti cheese
4 oz corned beef, thinly sliced
4 oz turkey breast, thinly sliced
Approx. 2 oz of sauerkraut
3 tbsp green chili, chopped and drained
Aioli garlic mustard sauce or deli mustard
Extra virgin olive oil

Pre-heat grill to medium. Brush lightly one side of slices of rye bread with olive oil and place on grill with bacon press on top until brown with dark grill marks. Remove from grill and assemble sandwich.

With toasted side to the inside, assemble in this order:
Turkey slices
First slice of cheese
Green chile
Sauerkraut
Corned beef slices
Second slice of cheese
Mustard as desired
Place second slice of bread on top and brush lightly with olive oil. Using bacon press on top, grill on each side until golden brown. Serve hot. Notes: Cooking time will vary depending on how high you place your grilling surface. I have also used sourdough bread with this recipe and it is delicious! Makes one great moist and messy sandwich!

Grilled Pizza

Ingredients for the Pizza Dough

Rick Keyes
Skaneateles, New York; Onondaga County

Now I do wish we lived closer so he could make these for me. I love a good pizza!

Makes 2 large pizzas or 4 thin pizzas

2 packages yeast
2 tsp sugar
4 cups of bleached flour
1 tsp salt
¼ cup extra virgin olive oil
1 + ½ cup of warm water

Put yeast and sugar in a cup. Add ½ cup of water. The water should be between 100 and 110 degrees F. Mix well. Let the yeast and sugar activate for about five minutes. In a large mixing bowl, add the flour, salt, olive oil, 1 cup of warm water and the yeast mixture. Mix well with a fork to get a smooth dough ball. Place a handful of flour on a mixing surface. Empty the contents of the bowl on to the flour and knead the dough for eight to ten minutes or until the texture is smooth and uniform. If the dough seems sticky, add a little more flour. To knead, push the dough ball with your hand onto the work surface, fold the dough and repeat the process. Your goal is to have a well mixed smooth dough ball. Place the dough in a bowl and drizzle with olive oil. Cover with a cloth. Let the dough rise for about an hour. Punch down the dough and wait about another 45 minutes. Successful dough is a result of time and patience!

Cut the dough in half. Coat a rolling pin with flour and gently shape dough on a floured mixing surface until the dough is the desired shape, depending on your cooking pan, rectangle or round. Keep using flour as needed so the dough won't stick. Use your hands to shape the dough or continue with a rolling pin. You want to end up with a dough shell ⅛ inch to ¼ inch thick. Dust a cookie sheet with flour or cornmeal. Oil will work ok, but the dough will be greasy. Slide the dough onto the cookie sheet. If you have a peel, assemble the pizza right on the peel dusted with cornmeal. Then use the peel to place the pizza on a pre-heated surface. You can also assemble the pizza first and then slide a peel underneath the pizza. If the pizza is sticky and won't slide easily, use some dental floss to slide under the dough!

The high, dry heat is perfect for pizza. As an alternative, you can use whole wheat flour. If you do, cut the yeast to one package.

Tomato Green Onion Pizza

Rick Keyes
Skaneateles, New York; Onondaga County

3 tbsp extra virgin olive oil
⅛ tsp salt
⅛ tsp cayenne pepper or liquid hot sauce (more or less to taste)
1 clove garlic, minced
2 tbsp fresh basil (2 tsp dried)
3 green onions or scallions, sliced
2 medium Roma tomatoes, chopped
1 cup shredded mozzarella cheese
2 oz feta cheese, crumbled
10 olives of your choice, cut in half

Combine oil, salt, pepper, and garlic together. Set aside 1 tablespoon, then add basil, onions and tomatoes to mixture and toss. Cover and let stand at room temperature for about 30 minutes to blend flavors. Preheat grill. Put prepared dough onto a floured surface. Carefully place dough on hot grill and heat for about one to two minutes or until it begins to brown. Remove dough from grill. Place browned side up and brush with the reserved olive oil mixture. Top with tomato mixture, cheeses and olives. Carefully return to grill. This is easier if you use a cookie sheet to carry the pizzas. Close lid and continue grilling for about two to four minutes or until bottom has browned and cheese is melted. Serve.

Anne Kinne

Grilled Feta and Tomato Pizza

Rick Keyes
Skaneateles, New York; Onondaga County

6 large Roma tomatoes, cut into thin slices (remember to use tomatoes that aren't overly ripe)
1 cup feta cheese
½ cup fresh basil, chopped
⅛ tsp cayenne pepper or pepper sauce (more or less to taste)
1 tsp salt
½ tsp black pepper
Extra virgin olive oil

Pre-cook one side of dough for two to three minutes. Remove from heat and set aside. Brush tomatoes with oil and grill on medium heat for one to two minutes, making sure not to turn them. Combine feta cheese with basil, salt, and black pepper. Place grilled tomatoes on the cooked side of pizza crust. Top off with feta cheese mixture. Place pizza back on the grill. Cook raw dough side for four minutes. Remove from heat and serve.

Scott's Pizza Theory

Scott Webb
San Diego, California: San Diego County

That's my cousin!

Pizza doesn't NEED a sauce to be flavorful, moist, and appealing. Be brave and try a pizza without any sauce or the traditional tomato sauce. Experiment with a creamy garlic sauce (find an Alfredo, or cheese/cream pasta sauce to use on pizza) or mustard pizza (see below).

Scott's Root Pizza

Use seasonal vegetables such as:
Potatoes, beets, carrots, onion and parsnips
Cut very thin
Sprinkle extra virgin olive oil on top of pizza to help it cook
Use any pizza dough you prefer

Scott's Mustard Pizza

Spread the mustard of your choice on a prepared pizza dough. Any mustard will do, from the fancy stone ground ones to the basic yellow. This will go well with toppings such as ham and cheese – again of your choice.

Scott's Refrigerator Cleaner Pizza

Being brave, check inside your refrigerator and use whatever is in the vegetable drawer to top a pizza. Caution: Don't use wet tomatoes. They make the pizza soggy.

Creamy Garlic Pizza

Anne Kinne
Pecos, New Mexico; Santa Fe County

2 cloves garlic, minced and mixed well with a cream sauce. I like to use an Alfredo sauce, from the pasta section of the grocery store.
Spread on top of the pizza dough of your choice

Top with:
Mozzarella cheese (depending on how big your pizza dough is, and how much you love cheese, I would use anywhere between 2 to 3 cups of cheese, since I'm a cheese lover)
1 to 2 cups chicken, grilled, baked, or any other cooked meat.
½ cup red onion, finely chopped
Place on grill and cook till cheese melts
Substitute cooked and drained sausage instead of the chicken, or in addition to the chicken.

12

Exotic Meats

Anne Kinne

Ostrich/Emu Filet

Rick Keyes
Skaneateles, New York; Onondaga County

2 tsp salt
Black pepper to taste
2 tsp dry mustard
6 ostrich filet steaks
1 clove garlic, chopped
¼ cup vinegar
¼ cup lemon juice
1 tsp grated lemon zest
2 tsp sugar
½ cup extra virgin olive oil

Mix salt, pepper to taste, and mustard in bowl. Rub mixture into steaks. Place meat in a dish. Mix garlic, vinegar, lemon juice, lemon zest, sugar and olive oil in separate bowl. Pour over meat and let marinate four hours, turning every hour. Grill steaks to desired doneness on barbecue.

Ostrich/Emu Burgers

Rick Keyes
Skaneateles, New York; Onondaga County

1 lb ground ostrich
2 tbsp onion, finely chopped
1 clove garlic, minced
1 tsp olive oil
1 tsp salt
½ tsp black pepper

Sauté onion and garlic in olive oil until slightly brown. Combine with other ingredients and form into patties about one inch thick. Preheat grill. Place patties on hot grill and cook on each side for four to five minutes or until done. Ostrich and emu can be eaten medium to medium-rare. Serve on buns with your favorite hamburger toppings.

Anne Kinne

Bison Burger

Rick Keyes
Skaneateles, New York; Onondaga County

9 oz ground bison meat (makes one patty)
½ tsp garlic salt
½ tsp ground black pepper
¼ tsp cayenne pepper (optional to taste)
¼ cup seasoned breadcrumbs
Cheese (optional)

Make into a patty. Season each side with spices. Place on grill and cook each side for just a few minutes, covered. Bison cooks fairly quickly so be careful not to overcook. For a medium-rare burger, cook for approximately four to five minutes.

Bison Steaks
Also used for Kobe Beef

Rick Keyes
Skaneateles, New York; Onondaga County

4 12 oz strip steaks (each about 1¼ inches thick), preferably Kobe (Wagyu)
3 tbsp olive oil, divided
2 tsp coarse kosher salt
2 tbsp very coarsely ground black pepper

Pre-heat grill. Pat steaks dry. Brush 1 tablespoon oil over both sides of steaks. Sprinkle with coarse salt and coarsely ground black pepper. Heat 1 tablespoon oil in heavy large skillet over high heat. Add steaks to skillet and cook for one minute per side to sear. Immediately move steaks to grill and cook over high heat about two minutes per side for rare to medium- rare (instant-read thermometer inserted into center of steaks registers 120 to 125 degrees F). Cover, keep warm, and let rest five minutes.

Grilled Venison Tenderloin

Rick Keyes
Skaneateles, New York; Onondaga County

1 lb venison tenderloin
1 cup red wine
1 clove minced garlic (fresh)
2 tbsp extra virgin olive oil
1 tsp soy sauce
1 tbsp ground black pepper
1 tsp salt
1 tbsp honey
Currant sauce

Trim meat. Remove all visible fat and most of the silver skin (translucent membrane). If loin has a long tapered end, curl the thin end back and tie in place. The goal is to have a uniform size to evenly cook. Mix together wine, olive oil, soy sauce, garlic and pepper and marinate in refrigerator one to two hours, turning meat occasionally, longer if meat is from an older animal. Start grill. Remove meat from marinade and pat dry. Bring to room temperature before grilling.

While grill heats, pour marinade into a small pan. Over high heat, cook down to about half of the original amount. Add honey and mix well, let cool to room temperature. Grill meat over direct heat, turning to brown all sides. Allow six to eight minutes per inch of thickness. Baste meat with reduced marinade twice during cooking process, and use remaining sauce when finished cooking. Use an instant-read thermometer (125 degrees F is medium-rare) or make a small cut to check doneness. Don't overcook or meat will be dry and tasteless. Let rest on warm platter a few minutes to distribute juices within the meat. Serve whole or sliced into 1 inch rounds with currant sauce.

Lamb Chops

Scott Webb
San Diego, California; San Diego County

3 to 4 chops per person, thick cut
1 cup extra virgin olive oil
2 tbsp fresh tarragon, chopped

Mix oil with tarragon to baste lamb. Place on grill, turning frequently and basting as you do. Use extra oil if needed to keep moist. Cook till done.
As an alternative to tarragon, substitute fresh sage.

Schmoul's Rack of Lamb

Schmoul
San Diego, California; San Diego County

Rack of lamb
Extra virgin olive oil
Herbs de Provence to taste
Rosemary to taste

Coat the whole thing in extra virgin olive oil. Sprinkle Herbs de Provence and rosemary to coat the lamb liberally. Sear it on both sides with a hot, hot fire, this locks in the juice. Pull it off the grill, separate the coals, place some soaked apple wood in a tray in the bottom of the grill. Place the lamb back on the grill with indirect heat. Do not use direct heat. If you have a gas grill, turn off one side of it to achieve indirect heat. Cook about 20 minutes or so till done. Close the grill and let it smoke. Do not overcook. Schmoul likes Herbs de Provence because it is a nice blend on the lamb. He will also just use extra virgin olive oil and garlic.

13

Side Dishes

Anne Kinne

Tony's Beans

Leslie Coridan
Riverside, California; Riverside County

Leslie recalls: "This is a piece of history at Sam Armstrong Realty from the 1980's. Sam Armstrong Realty is known today as Coldwell Banker Armstrong Properties and is in Riverside. I started at the company in 1985 and I am still there. There was a rather unique man by the name of Tony. He was quite a character. However, he loved to bring dishes to the office that won us all over. You never knew when you walked in the office what sort of an aroma would greet you. On the days that Tony brought in the crock pot filled with his wonderful beans, you just knew you had to have some. There was no question as to what that aroma was because you knew it was Tony's beans. Yum!"

1 lb ground round
1 lb bacon
1 lb ham (optional)
1½ lbs Italian sausage
3 cans beans - pinto, kidney, etc, (your choice)
28 oz catsup
14 oz or more barbecue sauce - Bulls Eye™ or KC Masterpiece™
3 medium onions
1 tbsp mustard
1 tbsp white vinegar
2 bell peppers (optional)

Put all ingredients in a six Qt crock pot and cook for at least six hours. Recipe can be used as a great potluck side dish or a main dish.

Dad's Gasless Beans – Ya Darn Tootin'

Demi Bowers Morrow
Walnut Creek, California; Contra Costa County

Demi explains: "The gasless beans are said with tongue in cheek—hence the 'ya darn tootin' remark! You could put a smile next to the title. I believe that dad talked to a chef in New Orleans about the recipe and then adjusted it to his own taste. I have the measurements that he used to serve 40 people with. He would cook them in our electric roaster. Yes, they were good, and he made them numerous times for huge crowds. In this day and age, I am not sure that anyone is interested in this long process, but that didn't daunt dad. He often tripled the recipe to serve at a Shrine event etc. The house sure smelled yummy while they were baking. They are good! Ya darn tootin!"

Serves 15 people

2 lbs Great Northern beans —soak overnight
1 big onion, cut up
1 lb brown sugar
1 tbsp dry mustard
¼ bottle of catsup
1½ tsp salt

Pour beans and water in which they were soaked into roaster, add other ingredients. Bake 12 hours at 250 degrees F. Water liquid should cover beans for at least the first ten hours.

Lisa's Heat of the Summer Salad

Lisa Hartman via Carol Youmans
San Diego, California; San Diego County

Lisa says: "This recipe is from my sister-in-law, Carol Youmans, who is an avid golfer. She had this salad at a golfing tournament and said this recipe *was the best part of her day. You can imagine how refreshing this is when coming off the course in Palm Springs in the heat of the summer!"*

4 cups watermelon, diced and seeded
2 cups jicama, diced
2 cups hot house cucumbers, diced
¼ cup each: basil, mint and cilantro, chopped
½ cup lime juice

Mix gently and serve cold.

Ensalada de Colores

Lisa Hartman
San Diego, California; San Diego County

It is a little known fact that Lisa lives about six blocks from where I used to live in the Ocean Beach Point Loma area of San Diego. She says: "Since I love to cook and am the hostess for our family gatherings, I am writing my own cookbook for my son Dan for when he leaves home. We have a lovely San Diego tropical backyard and we do a lot of grilling in the summer. I love color, so I like to cook with colorful foods that delight the senses. The recipes that I have included have spices like ginger and herbs that can be grown in our backyard."

Makes 5 cups

¼ cup extra virgin olive oil
¼ cup lime juice
1 tsp ground cumin
1½ cup jasmine rice
1 can black beans, rinsed
1 cup carrots, finely diced
¾ cup organic corn kernels
¾ cup tomato, finely chopped
¼ cup cilantro
¼ cup parsley
2 tbsp red onion, finely chopped
Salt and pepper to taste

In a serving bowl, blend olive oil, lime juice & cumin. Add other ingredients and mix gently. Season to taste.

Cabbage Salad Recipe - goes well with Kalbi

Holly Lamonica
San Diego, California; San Diego County

1 pkg Top Ramen™, chicken flavor, crushed (reserve seasoning packet for dressing)

4 green onions, chopped.

About 5 cups of cabbage, finely chopped or shredded

2 tbsp sesame seeds, toasted

½ slivered almonds, toasted

1 small can of mandarin oranges, drained.

1 cup cut up chicken breast, if desired

Mix, add dressing and refrigerate up to three hours before serving.

Dressing

¼ cup olive oil

2 tbsp lemon juice

½ tsp salt

1 tbsp salad vinegar

2 tbsp sugar

⅛ tsp ground ginger

1 packet of Top Ramen™ seasoning

Tri-Colored Pasta Salad

Micaela Jones
Nampa, Idaho; Ada County

My cousin of the "six degrees of separation" fame as noted in the marinades and sauces chapter. Thank you, 'Caela!

1 pkg tri-color pasta (spiral shape), cooked & cooled
1 cup feta cheese, crumbled
1 cup grape or cherry tomato, halved or quartered
1 cup cucumber, peeled and chopped
1 cup Greek olives, chopped, or canned sliced black olives will do
1 jar marinated artichoke hearts; reserve the oil
¼ cup red onion (optional), finely chopped
½ cup balsamic vinaigrette dressing

Toss all above ingredients together in a large bowl. When adding the dressing, you may want to add some of the artichoke marinade as well. Chill at least one hour (overnight is great) before serving.

Chile

Doris Kinne Lundy

I'm not real sure who Doris was. I found this recipe in my Grandmother Jesse's recipe box, so I know she was related.

1 large onion
2 tbsp butter
1 lb hamburger
1 Qt tomatoes
1 bunch celery
1 small can tomato soup
1 can kidney beans
Salt, pepper, and chili power (if desired) to taste

Cut onion in small pieces, sauté in butter in a large pan. To that, add the hamburger and cook until brown. Add the quart of tomatoes, the celery (chopped rather fine), and the small can of tomato soup. Continue to simmer to blend ingredients. Just before ready to serve, add the can of kidney beans.

Kuntry Potato Salad

Kathryn Christensen via Jan Christensen
Plentywood, Montana; Sheridan County and Albuquerque, New Mexico; Bernalillo County

Jan says: "This is one our favorites. It came from Ron's mother's recipes so I am sure that it came from Plentywood, Montana. It is very basic but keeps its zip."

4 cups cooked potatoes, diced
4 hard-boiled eggs, diced
¼ cup medium onions, diced
¾ cup salad dressing (AKA Miracle Whip™)
1¼ tsp salt
1 tbsp prepared mustard
¼ cup sugar
1¼ tbsp vinegar
Dab of milk

Combine potatoes, eggs, onion and celery. Mix together salad dressing, salt, mustard, sugar, vinegar and milk. Add to potato mixture, mixing just enough to cover. I used ½ cup sugar for 1½ recipe that serves eight to ten people. Double recipe for 12.

Grandma Dents' German Potato Salad

Grandma Dents via Kelli Christensen
Denver, Colorado; Jefferson County and Albuquerque, New Mexico; Bernalillo
County

Kelli remembers: "It's the one we've used in our family since I was a kid. Grandma Dents was a real German grandma, and a friend of mom's. We lived in Denver at the time."

5 large potatoes, boiled, peeled and chopped
2 large white onions, minced
1 raw egg
6 hard-boiled eggs, chopped
¾ cup vinegar
¾ cup sugar
Salt & pepper to taste
½ lb bacon, chopped fine & fried until brown

Add bacon to potatoes - no fat - and remove bacon fat from heat to cool slightly. Beat egg and add vinegar & sugar and add this mixture to the slightly cooled bacon fat, stirring as you pour it in. Be sure the bacon fat isn't too hot or you'll have a scrambled egg! Cook for a few minutes until the mixture thickens. Add to potatoes and mix together. Add 6 chopped hard-boiled eggs.

Baked Bean Casserole

Kathryn Christensen via Jan Christensen
Plentywood, Montana; Sheridan County and Albuquerque, New Mexico; Bernalillo County

Jan says: "This recipe was given to me by my mother-in-law. I'm not sure what a 2½ can is, but I always buy a really big one [of pork and beans]."

Serves 10-12

1 #2 ½ can pork and beans, not drained
1 can chili beans
1 can kidney beans, drained
1 can cut green beans, drained
1 medium onion, chopped fine
½ cup vinegar
½ cup brown sugar
2 tbsp prepared mustard
5 or 6 strips bacon, slightly cooked

Place all the beans in a large bowl. Mix the vinegar, brown sugar, mustard and onion together and add to the beans. Place in two-and-a-half Qt casserole dish and cover with 5 to 6 strips of bacon. Bake 1½ hours at 350 degrees F.

Anne Kinne

Blue Cheese Coleslaw

Nan Perkins
Goodyear, Arizona; Maricopa County

My cousin Nan is another of the best cooks in the family.

Slaw
2 lbs Napa cabbage, shredded
8 oz blue cheese, crumbled (I used gorgonzola)
¼ cup green onions (white part and some of the green), chopped

Dressing
¾ cup vegetable oil
⅓ cup cider vinegar
2 tbsp sugar
1 tsp celery seeds
2 garlic cloves, minced
½ tsp salt
½ tsp white pepper
¼ tsp dry mustard

Whisk the dressing until it is mixed well. I make the dressing and chop the cabbage the day before. Toss the cabbage, blue cheese and green onions. Pour over the slaw mixture just before serving. It will become wilted if you add the dressing ahead of time.

Lemon Syrup for Lemonade

Tobianne Neal via Nan Perkins
Ohio via Goodyear, Arizona; Maricopa County

1 cup water
2½ cups sugar
Cook sugar and water until sugar dissolves, stirring constantly

Add:
Pinch of salt
Zest from 4 lemons

Boil five minutes. Remove from heat and cool. Add 3 cups fresh lemon juice and refrigerate. Stir thoroughly before making lemonade. Mix 3 water to 1 syrup for lemonade. Can divide up cooled syrup and freeze for later. Very, *very* good!

Anne Kinne

Jeanne's Potato Salad

Pecos, New Mexico; San Miguel County

Jeanne recalls: "My mom would make this a lot for summer barbecues or picnics. She would always mix the ingredients, except the onion. She would put some in a separate bowl for me, and add onion to the rest. Guess who doesn't like onions?" I can vouch for that!

6 potatoes, boiled, cooled, peeled, and cut into cubes
4 hard-boiled eggs, diced
3 stalks celery, finely chopped
½ cup mayo
¼ cup mustard
Vinegar, salt, paprika to taste
3 halves dill pickles, finely chopped
¼ cup sweet relish
Chopped onion if desired
Paprika sprinkled on top of finished salad

Mix all ingredients together. Should be tasted after mixed together. I always have to add something more, like dill pickles. Jeanne does like her pickles!

Jeanne's Deviled Eggs

Pecos, New Mexico; San Miguel County

Her claim to fame: "On any family get-together, I am always required to bring the deviled eggs. I always have to be careful when my sons are around because, if I turn my back on them, the eggs are gone. My brother-in-law won't eat any deviled eggs except mine."

6 hard-boiled eggs
2 tbsp mayo
1 tsp vinegar or more to taste
1 tsp mustard
½ tsp salt
Dash pepper and paprika

Slice eggs lengthwise. I like to use a serrated knife because it makes a design. Mix egg yolks with other ingredients, mixing thoroughly. Fill egg whites with mixture and sprinkle paprika on top.

Anne Kinne

Potato Salad

Diann Leach
San Antonio, Texas; Bexar County

Diann speaks: "My mother said one 'good-size' potato for two people. Adjust sugar, vinegar, and mustard to taste. I try to make the dressing a day ahead and let sit in refrigerator to 'season.' I'll even try to cut up veggies etc. the day ahead, doesn't make it so tiring when putting together. Mother added cut up cucumbers to her salad, but Jerry doesn't care for them."

4 potatoes, cooked with skins on, drained and cooled. Cut into cubes
⅓ or so cup onion
¾ to 1 tsp celery seed
Salt and pepper to taste

Cover and let sit overnight in refrigerator.

Add chopped celery, radishes, shredded carrots and one chopped hard-boile egg per person. All this is to desired taste.

Dressing
Depends on quantity of salad you're making

For the above amounts use:
3 cups mayonnaise
2 tbsp mustard
1 tsp sugar
1 tsp apple cider vinegar

Karen's Baked Beans

Karen Leach via Diann Leach
San Antonio, Texas; Bexar County

3 cans pork 'n beans
¼ cup chopped onion
2 tbsp Worcestershire Sauce
½ cup catsup
½ cup barbecue sauce
¼ cup brown sugar

Bake at 350 degrees F for two hours.
Can put bacon pieces on top.

Onion Baked Beans

Anita Kilgore
Pecos, New Mexico; San Miguel County

2 cans pork and beans
1 pouch dry onion soup mix
4 slices bacon
2 tbsp maple flavored syrup

In a two Qt casserole dish, combine beans, soup mix and syrup. Arrange bacon on beans. Bake at 350 degrees F for one hour or until hot and bubbling

Grilled Potatoes

Anne Kinne
Pecos, New Mexico; Santa Fe County

Makes 4 servings

2 to 3 large potatoes, washed and cut into 1 inch cubes
1 medium onion, diced
Garlic salt or powder (optional) or 1 to 2 cloves of fresh garlic, finely minced
Salt and pepper to taste
Butter

In a large bowl, thoroughly mix cubed potatoes with diced onion. Season with garlic, salt and pepper. Take four sheets of aluminum foil, about 12 inches or so, and lay them on the counter. Equally divide up potato mixture between the four foil sheets. Dab with butter. Close tightly. Place on grill over indirect heat. Cook till done.

Grilled Potatoes Take Two

Jan Meslin
Mission Veijo, California; Orange County

From her Scouting days, Jan remembers this yummy campfire recipe that we probably all have tasted.

Using the above recipe for grilled potatoes add:
1 lb cooked ground beef
3 carrots, sliced

Make the foil pouches larger than 12 inches and cook over indirect heat till done.

Grilled Corn on the Cob

Anne Kinne
Pecos, New Mexico; Santa Fe County

I do NOT like to have the corn silk impede my enjoyment of corn on the cob, which is why I thoroughly clean it before I cook it. It is easier for me to do this while the corn is cold, rather than to do it after it is cooked.

Corn
Butter

Husk the corn, and remove the silk. You can find a corn/silk cleaning brush in many stores to help with this task. Place each ear of corn in a sheet of foil. Dab liberally with butter. Grill on indirect heat for approximately 20 minutes till done, turning frequently.

Grilled Corn on the Cob Take Two

Scott Webb
San Diego, California; San Diego County

Soak corn in water with the husk still intact for a half hour or so.

Place on grill over indirect heat, and cook till done, turning frequently.

Grilled Corn on the Cob Take Three

Dave Kilgore
Santa Fe, New Mexico; Santa Fe County

Dave goes fishing at many a New Mexico Lake, as noted above. When he goes north to Heron Lake, he stays in a cabin without a refrigerator. To keep the corn cold, he throws ice in a large plastic bag, and puts the corn in there. As the ice melts, the corn is then soaking in water. Dave can spend days at this cabin, fishing to his heart's content, and keeping the corn fresh!

Soak corn in water with the husk still intact for up to 24 hours. Open husk, spread liberally with butter, close and place on grill over indirect heat, and cook till done, turning frequently.

Anne Kinne

Schmoul's Beans

Schmoul
San Diego, California; San Diego County

Here we go with yet another of Schmoul's fantastic creations! Be careful with this one, Schmoul likes his beans hot!

1 can black beans
1 can Great Northern white beans
1 can kidney beans
2 cans Texas ranch jalapeno beans (this is the base)
You can include more of any of the beans, depending on how many people you're making this for.
Rinse the beans, but not the Texas beans. Keep the juice.
5 or 6 cloves of garlic
1 whole onion, minced
A few multi-colored peppers, yellow, orange, red, green
Serrano chilies (seeded) – *careful with these. Wash your hands thoroughly after touching them and, under no circumstances, touch your eyes until your hands are completely free of their fire!*
Fresh julienne ginger, a whole handful, the more you use the hotter it will be
Fresh cilantro

Sauté the onion, garlic, ginger, peppers, and a couple Serrano chilies in a very large pot. Put the beans on top of that, bring to barely a simmer. Once it's hot, just before it's served, take a whole huge bunch of minced cilantro and stir in. If it's a big bunch of beans, take two bunches of cilantro. Schmoul likes his cilantro!

Overnight Alfalfa-Celery Salad

Gratia Berggren via Dean Berggren
Lewistown, Ohio; Logan County via Lakewood, Colorado; Jefferson County

½ lb alfalfa sprouts
1½ cups green onion, chopped
2 cups celery, chopped
1 (8 oz) can sliced water chestnuts, drained
1 (10 oz) package frozen peas, thawed
2 cups mayonnaise
2 tsp sugar
½ tsp salt
½ tsp pepper
1 cup (4 oz) shredded mozzarella cheese
½ cut grated Parmesan cheese
Tomato wedges for garnish
Dried parsley flakes

Layer alfalfa sprouts, green onion, celery, water chestnuts, and peas in a four Qt bowl. Combine mayonnaise, sugar, salt, and pepper. Mix well. Spread over top, sealing to edge of bowl. Combine cheese, and sprinkle over top. Cover tightly, and chill 24 hours. At serving time, arrange tomato wedges around edge of bowl. Sprinkle the salad with parsley flakes.

Anne Kinne

Grilled Rosemary Potatoes

Anne Kinne
Pecos, New Mexico; Santa Fe County

4 red potatoes (or Yukon Gold), washed and cubed
4 or so sprigs of fresh rosemary
Butter

Cut four lengths of foil and lay them on the counter. Place equal amounts of potato on each piece of foil. Break each sprig of rosemary in half, placing each half in the middle of each pile of potato. Top with a couple dabs of butter, close tightly. Place on grill, over indirect heat. Cook till done.

Jean's Potato Salad

Jean Kinne Maurer via Anne Kinne
San Diego, California; San Diego County via Pecos, New Mexico; Santa Fe County

This is my mom's recipe. There are so many potato salad recipes floating around in our family, you could lose count!

Serves 4 to 6

I used to use brown russet potatoes until my cousin Micaela said to try the white potatoes. She was right! They do hold their shape better.
4 large white potatoes, cubed then boiled till done
1 medium onion, finely chopped
1½ tsp celery seed

Mix above ingredients well the day before. Cover tightly and store overnight in refrigerator. Also, the day before you serve this, you can put together:

2 or 3 carrots, washed and chopped fine
1 or 2 stalks celery, washed and chopped fine
4 or 5 radishes, washed and chopped fine

The above ingredients can be stored separately in Ziploc™ baggies overnight in refrigerator.

1 dozen hard-boiled eggs

On the day you serve the salad: Combine the potato – onion mixture with the carrots, celery and radishes in a LARGE bowl. Mix slowly and gently so as not to mash the potatoes. Salt and pepper to taste. Add 4 to 6 hard-boiled eggs, finely chopped, mixing gently.

Dressing
In a separate bowl, start with 2 cups of mayonnaise mixed with ½ cup Miracle Whip™. Mix thoroughly. Add in sugar to taste. Start with one tsp and check for taste. Add more sugar if needed. Continue to taste until desired blending is reached. I like a smooth, non-sharp flavor. Pour over potatoes and vegetables, gently and slowly so the potatoes don't lose their shape. Use as much dressing as needed for desired "wetness" of salad. Garnish with remaining hard-boiled eggs, cut lengthwise in quarters. Sprinkle paprika on top and serve.

Anne Kinne

Auntie Winn's Coleslaw

Winnifred Schroeder
Previously of San Diego, California; currently of Austin, Texas; Travis County

1½ lbs cabbage, shredded
1 carrot, grated
¼ green pepper, chopped

Mix with dressing made as follows:
½ envelope (scant) Italian dressing
½ cup sour cream or buttermilk
½ cup mayonnaise
¼ cup sugar
2 tbsp vinegar

Best if made early in the morning of the day you serve it. I always love Auntie Winn's notes on her recipe cards. On this one, she uses the word "scant," which means not a whole. The Italian seasoning may have been too much for her palate when she used a full half envelope.

Auntie Winn's Potato Salad

Winnifred Schroeder
Previously of San Diego, California; currently of Austin, Texas; Travis County

Serves 6

4 to 5 potatoes, depending on size
1 small onion, diced
1 tsp celery seed
1 stalk celery (more if desired), diced

1 egg per person and 1 for top garnish, hard-boiled and cooled
¼ green or red pepper (optional), diced

Day before using:
Salt and boil, cool and peel potatoes. Cut into ½ inch pieces. Mix with onion, celery and celery seed. Cover and refrigerate overnight.

The next day:
Mix with eggs, cut up, and pepper

Dressing
Mix ¾ cup Miracle Whip™ with ½ cup mayonnaise (or mix half and half)
Salt and a dash of pepper
1 tsp to 1 tbsp mustard (depending on your taster)
¼ cup sweet relish

Pour over salad and mix well.

Grilled Baked Potatoes

Dave Kilgore
Santa Fe, New Mexico; Santa Fe County

Dave likes to pierce the potato before he microwaves it halfway through. Place on the grill wrapped in aluminum foil. Do not use butter to coat it. Resist the temptation till the spud is finished. Cook till done. The skin turns out really crispy with this method, something Dave likes a lot!

As an alternative, place the potato (pierced first) on the grill wrapped in foil. Cook the entire time on the grill. Do not use butter with this method either.

Grilled Squash

Dave Kilgore
Santa Fe, New Mexico; Santa Fe County

Any kind of squash you like – cut in cubes
Dab with butter
Salt, pepper, and garlic to taste

Mix well, place in foil pouch. Place on grill and cook till desired tenderness.

Stampede Party Deviled Eggs Yahoo! Guaranteed to Stop a Bull in its Tracks!

Sandra Anderson
Calgary, Alberta, Canada

These are famous up in Canada and in America! I always guesstimate the number of guests and plan on at least two deviled eggs per person with a few extra.

Eggs - I buy extra large, fresh brown eggs
Red onions
Fresh dill
Fresh leeks
Paprika
Mayonnaise
Stuffed pimento olives
Small pickled onions
Cupcake papers (I like themes so plan on colors to suit the occasion)
Paprika
Lemon pepper (No MSG)
Sea salt

Egg Preparation
Boil eggs for four to five minutes, keeping a sharp eye on the time. Check to see if they are ready by slicing one egg in half. The yolk will be hard and dry. Do not overcook or the yolk will turn black and it will not be usable.

Once ready, run under lukewarm water, cracking the shells a little, and begin to peel off the shells. Cracking the top of an egg (small concave space) allows you to get the shell off without damaging the egg (usually!). There will be some that refuse to cooperate so make allowance for those little devils by cooking a few extra. Once all are peeled and cooling, immediately slice lengthwise and extract the yolk into a large mixing bowl. Rinse any remaining yolk from the half-egg shells and place on paper towel to dry.

Olives & Pickled Onions (This is Important!)

- drain bottle(s) of olives and onions
- wrap in paper towels. You will have to do this more than once. They must be very dry as any juice will ruin your eggs!

Chop up very fine the red onion, leeks and dill. Do not use too much

dill.
Wash everything carefully in hot water to avoid any contamination, especially in the layers of the leeks. Dry all in paper towels. Must all be very dry.

In a blender, mix in the egg yolks, red onion, leeks, dill, lemon pepper (to taste), sea salt (not much – the olives and onions are also salty) and mayonnaise. Just a minute or two to mix it well. You want to end up with a texture that is not too runny but not too hard either. I often find that I add more mayo as I am blending as I want the finished product to harden in the refrigerator overnight.

Fill each half-egg with the filling, add an olive (end to end as you want the pimento to add color to your creation) or the onion (capers could be added – two or three to a toothpick). Dust lightly with paprika.

Place each egg in a cupcake paper on a tray to be placed in the refrigerator. I use a baking sheet as I want to maximize space in the refrigerator. Cover tray with Saran Wrap™ and make sure it is tight so that no air can get in. Otherwise your eggs will dry out overnight and look, well, nasty! Keep in the refrigerator until just before serving. I do not put all out at once. Replenish the table as time goes on.

Anne Kinne

14

Condiments

Anne Kinne

Best Pickles in the World

Frances Wemple Bowers
Fargo, North Dakota; Cass County

Soak large (6 inches long or more) cucumbers in very cold or ice water for five hours. Cut lengthwise without paring into about five pieces. Pack very closely into Qt jars with 3 stalks celery and 3 slices of onion to each jar.

Drain off any juice after packing.

Heat together:
1 Qt vinegar
1 cup sugar
½ cup water
⅓ cup salt.

Boil well. Pour over cucumbers. Seal at once. Ready for use in four weeks.

"Tomato Ketchup"

Ida Christopherson; ca 1900
Fergus Falls, Minnesota; Otter Tail County

Don't you just love the spelling?

3 gallons tomatoes
6 onions
6 red peppers
1 tsp celery seed
2 tsp mustard seed

Boil 20 minutes. Run through colander and boil down some.

Second cooking
2 tsp whole cloves
1 box stick cinnamon
2½ cups vinegar
3 tbsp salt
2 cups sugar

Boil till thick enough. Remove the cloves and cinnamon sticks. Bottle.

Gratia's Candied Dills

Gratia Berggren via Dean Berggren
Lewistown, Ohio; Logan County via Lakewood, Colorado; Jefferson County

½ gallon jar dill pickles cut in 1
inch slices
3 cups sugar
1 cup cider vinegar
1 tsp celery seed
2 tsp mustard seed
1 sm. stick cinnamon
½ tsp ground allspice

Boil ingredients together and cool.
Pour over drained and cut up dill
pickles. Let stand 24 hours and then
refrigerate.

Mother's Pepper Relish

Jesse Kinne to Gratia Berggren via Dean Berggren
Fergus Falls, Minnesota; Otter Tail County to Lewistown, Ohio; Logan County via
Lakewood, Colorado; Jefferson County

12 green peppers
9 red peppers
15 onions

3½ cups sugar
1 Qt vinegar
1 tbsp salt

Remove all seeds from peppers, grind. Place in large bowl and pour boiling water (amount doesn't matter, but just enough to cover them) over them. Let stand 15 minutes and drain. Place in large pot. To that add:

Cook slowly for 45 minutes. This will fill 12 eight oz jars and four odd jars (not 8 oz).

Anne Kinne

15

Dessert

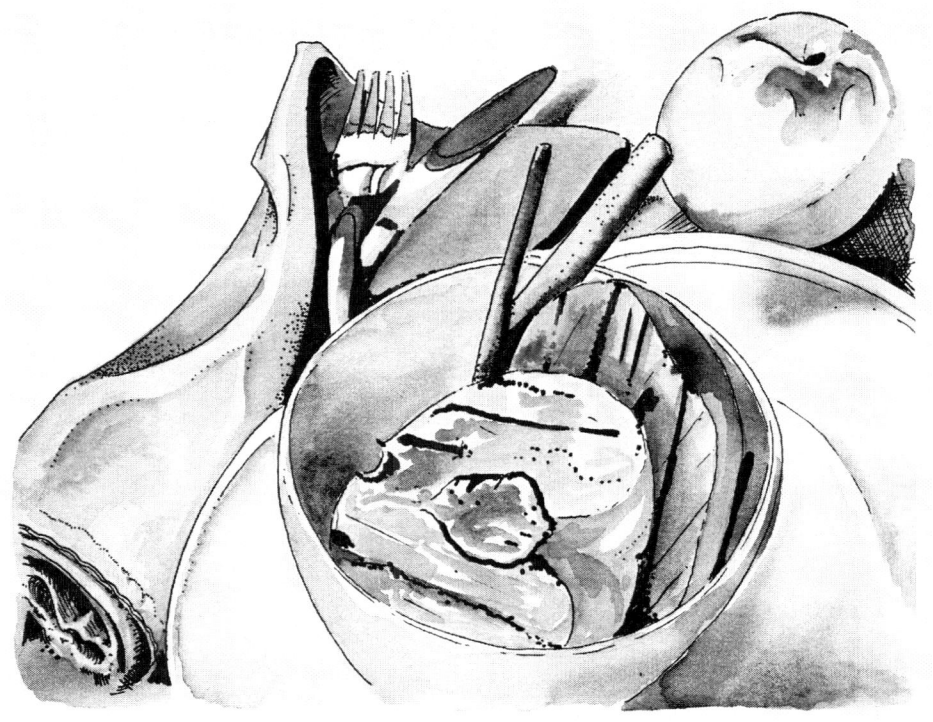

Anne Kinne

Banana Boats

Jan Meslin
Mission Veijo, California, Orange County

Slice banana lengthwise (keep peel on)
Insert about 20 chocolate chips

Close up and wrap in foil. Place on grill for a couple of minutes.

Grilled Pineapple

Cathryne Richards
Placitas, New Mexico; Sandoval County

Cathryne remembers living in Hawaii: "We grilled pineapple every day while we were in Hawaii. It is a real simple and sweet dessert and goes with everything, and, while I can't eat very much raw pineapple, this is terrific day after day."

Choose a ripe pineapple - gold are best

Peel and slice into ½ inch slices and place on grill

Turn over and rotate ¼ turn to produce cross-mark grill strips

Grill only about three minutes on each side.

Anne Kinne

16

Calling All Recipes for 2009

Do you have a recipe that you would like to see included in the next book?

Just send an e-mail with your recipe in a word document or PDF to:

recipes@CoastToCoastBbq.com

You can also mail your recipe to:

Coast to Coast BBQ 2009
R. Keyes
PO Box 527
Skaneateles NY 13152

Those sending in recipes that are included in the Coast to Coast BBQ 2009 edition will receive a free book.

Be sure to include your name, address, and telephone number when submitting recipes.

About The Author

Anne has been cooking for over thirty years. It took, however, a move to rural Humboldt County, California for her to wean herself off of fast food. There was only one drive thru in the town where she lived, which by necessity got her serious cooking creative juices flowing. Living even more rurally now, she relies on her creative prowess and what happens to be in stock in her kitchen at any given moment. Inventive by nature, she loves to experiment, rarely measures amounts of ingredients, and gets pleasure from being in the kitchen with others while preparing meals. She lives in the Sangre de Cristo Mountains of Northern New Mexico with her two cats, a dog, and her trusty grill.

Notes

Notes

Notes

Anne Kinne

Notes

Notes

Notes